Listen Chicano!

do you know what a
'stereotype' is?

Foreword: Barry M. Goldwater U.S. Senator, Arizona

Illustrations: Joseph Wortman

Listen Chicano!

An Informal History of the Mexican-American

Manuel A. Machado, Jr.

Nelson Hall nh Chicago

Library of Congress Cataloging in Publication Data

Machado, Manuel A.
    Listen Chicano!

    Bibliography: p.
    Includes index.
    1. Mexican Americans—History. I. Title.
E184.M5M25   973'.04'6872   77-16650
ISBN 0-88229-258-7 (cloth)
ISBN 0-88229-560-8 (paper)

Str. 15.95 8.00 10/4/78

Manufactured in the United States of America

I sincerely dedicate this book to the following:

Friends—Terry Cunningham, James T. Judge, Donald M. Dozer, Philip W. Powell, Lawrence Kinnaird, Raúl Castro.

Family—Marcy, Anna, Paul, Alicia, Travis, Mr. and Mrs. Manual Machado, Sr., Mrs. Eloisa Saba.

Critters—The profusion of horse, cat, dog, and goat flesh is too long. Suffice it to say they too can have a piece of the action.

Contents

Forword/**ix**   *by Senator Barry M. Goldwater*

Introduction/**xi**

PART I

1. Legacies in Conflict/**1**
2. Cultures at Loggerheads/**15**
3. Adaptation and Conflict,
   Mexican-Americans and Anglos, 1848–1910/**31**
4. Revolutions, Migrants, and Depression,
   1910–1940/**51**
5. Braceros, Riots, and
   Awakening Consciousness, 1940–1960/**73**

PART II

Introduction/**95**

6. Grapes and Turf: *La Huelga* and the Land
   Grant Dispute/**97**
7. The Mexican-American and
   the Socio-Political Order/**115**
8. Academia and Riots/**135**
9. Cultural Schizophrenia/**153**
10. A Summing Up/**177**
    Bibliography/**185**

Index/**193**

Foreword

Having been born, literally, on the Mexican border—I've held a lifelong interest, not only in the Mexican citizen, but in the American citizen of Mexican extraction. The real story of this wonderful group of people has long needed telling, and I'm very happy that Manuel Machado, a native Arizonan, has undertaken the work. In fact, he allowed me to read quite a bit of it before he had finished it, and I'm extremely impressed with the way he has presented his own people.

Without Mexico, I don't know what the southwestern part of the United States would be—not just from the standpoint of the culture; the language; the names of our towns, streets, and counties—but from the great addition to our citizenry that the American with Mexican lineage has brought to us. In my state, they serve at all levels of government and at all levels of industry and the professions, and they are very, very highly respected and regarded.

Unfortunately, of late, some politicians with national ambitions have been attempting to cause disputes amongst these people so that they would take sides in a political way—supposedly for their own good. The true Mexican-Americans—and I avoid using the word Chicano because when I was a boy, to call a Mexican-American a Chicano was a guaranteed way to get into a fight—are dedicated Americans who bring this dedication from the homeland, Mexico.

I have always honestly believed that the Mexican has a greater attachment to and understanding of the word freedom than we Anglos who live north of the border. They have brought this with them to the United States, and they have demonstrated this by the fact that probably the greatest source of men for our fighting forces comes from families with Mexican names.

I congratulate Mr. Machado on his work, and I know that the reader is going to find it extremely interesting.

Barry M. Goldwater,
United States Senator,
Arizona

Introduction

From the outset, the preparation of a personal analysis of the historical evolution of the Mexican-American proved formidable and at first impossible. Why? God knows other scholars have tackled equally thorny questions, loaded with statistical data, fraught with politico-economic nuances, and leading the researcher down the perilous road of supercaution and timidity in things academic and intellectual. Perhaps it results from pent-up rebelliousness, for woe to he who generalizes without pages of redundant data to substantiate even the most minor conclusion! A pox on the *pobre cristiano* who might consciously put himself out on an intellectual limb because he gave recognition to his experiences and conditioning during the preparation of his work. While certainly the more general approach makes itself more susceptible to criticism, at the same time it is really a lot more fun. Moreover, in this business we need to have some fun with our work rather than surrender to the sterility of the footnote and the guarded phrase.

The late Herbert Eugene Bolton once declared that history should, above all else, be fun. It should, in effect, afford the mind an opportunity to play with data and ideas, to treat history as an aesthetic experience rather than subjugating the matrix of both the social sciences and the humanities to the impotence of scientism.

It seems, therefore, that the history of the Mexican-American lends itself to playful treatment. For one thing it helps alleviate some of the deadly seriousness of the ideologues and their dreadful statistics. Statistical material becomes a vehicle from which generalizations are drawn rather than entities unto themselves whereby one might, if sufficiently perspicacious, infer certain conclusions. Secondly, breaking the shackles of historical convention occasionally allows the historian to eliminate an excess of splenetic juices and thereby averts a potential duodenal or pyloric ulcer. Thirdly, and probably of greatest import in a personal sense, it allows for the restoration of history to some semblance of literary art. History can, at least sporadically, emerge from the morass of scientific jargon, psychiatric mumbo-jumbo, and computerized obscenities that serve no purpose other than to bemuse and befuddle; *humanitas* in history can, therefore, elevate the Muse to the reigning queen of the humanities and social sciences and not leave her in the role of Academic Cinderella. Perhaps the homely adage found in some taverns in the frozen steppes of Western Montana might prove applicable: "If you can't dazzle 'em with brilliance, baffle 'em with bullshit!" Perhaps so, providing that the aforementioned pasture pie is, like the poetry of Luis de Góngora, constituted of some beneficent substance and not merely smell. With that, let us have a romp through the history of the Mexican-American.

Introduction Proper

Listen, Chicano! A battle cry emerged in the Southwest and in California calling the Mexican-American to join against the Anglos in an attempt to recoup alleged losses of the past three hundred years. The Anglo has oppressed you, the Anglo has robbed you, the Anglo has stolen your dignity as a man and as a Mexican. Therefore, rally against the continuation of a system that negates your culture and oppresses your body and overthrow the shackles of Anglo imperialism. Lord save us from the propagandists!!

Such calls to battle become more and more strident throughout the Southwest and California. The Mexican-American is an awakening minority, becoming aware of its potential as a political and economic force, and the imperative of organization makes necessary a resort to demagoguery of the basest sort. The demagoguery of the Mexican-American militant attempts to polarize all Mexican-Americans into a single ethnic unit and subsequently organize this group into a viable political force. Such a maneuver bases itself upon a series of assumptions that convert the Mexican-American into a homogeneous unit in which all members respond in similar if not identical fashion to a given set of stimuli.

The first of these assumptions, unfortunately, is that of ethnic homogeneity. It is assumed that the Mexican-American comprises a single socio-economic unit. This belief, often held sacrosanct by both Anglos and militant Chicanos, fails to take into account the historical complexity of Mexican-American evolution. There exists a patent failure to recognize the vast cultural and economic differences extant within the Mexican-American community today.

Moreover, the homogeneity myth is fed by the lack of scholarly investigation about the Mexican-American. With the exception of some industrious anthropologists who studied family life in Mexican-American communities, very little work has been done to analyze the role of the Mexican-American in the life of the United States. No generally accepted historical periods exist, and as a result, difficulties arise in an attempt to place this group in perspective. Scholarly investigators instead bare their bleeding hearts and join the hue and cry for Chicano solidarity and Brown Power while at the same time flagellating themselves with mea culpas.

Divisions within the Mexican-American community further destroy ethnic cohesiveness. Mexican-Americans often do not like the term Mexican-American. If they are descended from the old stock that participated in the initial settlement of the Southwest and California, Mexican denotes a lower class status. Waves of immigration from Mexico since 1848 exacerbated further the divisions between old families and new arrivals.

In addition, as some Mexican-Americans progressed up the socio-economic ladder, they blended more and more with the ultimately dominant Anglo culture. Mexican-Americans are represented in all levels of society, and their socio-economic positions condition their responses more than any sort of amorphous appeal to ethnicity.

As if ethnic solidarity were not enough, the new Chicano militancy declares a racial solidity. Such a declaration negates absolutely the hybridized racial stock that is in fact Mexican. The Mexican-American is told that his primary racial stock is Indian and not Spanish. His heroes are Mexico's Indian heroes. Spanish glory and achievement become, for the Mexican-American, an ugly story of oppression and subjugation of Mexico's Indian people. Nonsense!!

In the last ten years the Mexican-American emerged as a power to be reckoned with in the Southwest and in California. In New Mexico, the Mexican-American, who comprises approximately 40 percent of the population, received political sops. Dennis Chávez for years served as United States Senator from that state. Upon his death, Joseph Montoya went to Washington. In Texas, Congressman Henry González represents San Antonio. Yet, the last decade has seen the Mexican-American organize and become a force at the local level.

Mexican-Americans now sit on school boards in Los Angeles, in Texas towns, and in communities throughout the Southwest. City councilmen in many areas now have Spanish surnames. All of this adds up to an imperative for consideration.

[handwritten margin note: political power ✳]

Into the breach steps the academician and the bleeding heart liberal, terms that occasionally might interchange without loss of meaning. Awareness by liberal spirits of restlessness in the barrios means that programs and agencies must be organized to compensate for the centuries(??!!) of wrongdoing by the Anglos. An orgy of self-mortification begins. Suddenly the Mexican-American becomes a "problem" to be studied but not necessarily understood. We must, proclaim the suddenly interested academics and liberals, care for our little brown brethren of barrio and field. We must give to them the benefits of the American way of life. We must eliminate those things in their existence that keep them from becoming full and active participants in the American way. In short, we must have "gringoized" Mexicans, fitting into some sort of arbitrary cultural mold.

Such ego flagellation becomes, at best, disgusting, for there is no attempt to understand the diverse cultural backgrounds that comprise the somewhat inchoate group called the Mexican-American. Instead, the Anglo reformer, like the Chicano militant, grasps at the idea of cultural and racial homogeneity and attempts to force the Mexican-American into an arbitrary slot.

Admittedly, the vast majority of the evidence on the Mexican-American remains to be unearthed. Yet, it shall stay subsumed in archives and statistical tables until a modicum of rationality is restored and visceral, conditioned responses become aberrations instead of accepted hypotheses.

In all probability, the best approach to the study of the Mexican-American lies in the area of comparative history. The vast majority of the Mexican-American population inhabits a strip of land approximately two hundred miles north of the Mexican border in the Southwest and California. This political boundary, however, does not divide sharply the cultures that have fused in that region. As a result, the blending of cultures in the Southwest and in California necessitates analyses of those cultural components that have blended as well as conflicted when diverse cultural groups came into contact with each other.

This personalized essay will attempt to suggest some of those elements that need study before the Mexican-American can be viewed with any sort of perspective. As a Mexican-American, it offends me to receive condescension from Anglo colleagues and associates. Yet, their attitudes are, in a sense, predictable because they have no perspective in which to view the Mexican-American. A broadened mind would certainly be more liberal than one that operated on a given set of assumptions.

Orchids, Kudos, and Brickbats

In the preparation of any sort of manuscript, more people than the author become involved. Family, colleagues, friends, and antagonists all play a major though often unbeknownst role in the writing of the work. Positively, of course, my family—one wife, four children, seven horses, seven (damn it, eight—we just added one) cats, two dogs, and two goats—supported my efforts while the typewriter plinked away for hours on end. The children believed their father was an electrical instrument, my wife euphemistically referred to me as an "old bear," and the various and sundry beasties of house, pen, and pasture probably welcomed the neglect in their respective training schedules. Now that the work is completed, I can turn my attention to family affairs once again. Therefore, to my family I give thanks for their support and understanding in this endeavor.

To friends, colleagues, and students who read the manuscript in the various stages, I give thanks for their suggestions and comments. I especially would like to thank James T. Judge, Linda Sue Frey, Ross Toole, Joseph Wortman, Anthony Beltramo and a plethora of graduate and undergraduate students—past and present—for their comments and reactions. They, of course, are absolved of errors that might remain.

A special vote of thanks goes to Joseph Wortman for the excellent illustrations in the work. He definitely captured the essence of the manuscript and skillfully conveyed his impressions to paper.

Also deserving of special thanks is Senator Barry Goldwater of Arizona. His foreword to this work gave me impetus to carry on in the groves of academe, despite some of the attendant nonsense of the academy. To Senator Goldwater I owe a special gratitude for his unflinching belief in individual worth rather than any sort of "groupie" consciousness. Senator Goldwater is a fighter for individualism. In my youthful student days—long before he and I became acquainted—his writings and statements encouraged me to stick to my guns on various issues. For this I am especially grateful.

At a more intimate level, I luckily was the student of four men at the University of California, Santa Barbara, who buttressed the Senator's attitudes and encouraged me to persevere. They are Donald M. Dozer, Philip W. Powell, Lawrence Kinnaird, and Henry Adams. These men primarily guided my graduate studies between 1961 and 1964, and they, therefore, must indirectly share the responsibility for what they wrought. To them go many thanks.

To be sure, my parents also shoulder the blame for the work. They produced the author and encouraged his various endeavors throughout school and beyond. Thanks to them can never be expressed completely.

Also, my good friend Governor Raúl Castro of Arizona must also get thanks merely because he is a friend. His perseverance and integrity mark him as an exemplar for other Mexican-Americans not yet deluded by the ethnic blinkers of the militantas. To *mi amigo Raúl, le extiendo por esta página un abrazo.*

If Senator Goldwater, Governor Castro, former professors, students, family, and parents proved to be positive influences, one should also be thankful for the negative side of things, for this provides the necessary contrasts that clarify one's thinking on various issues. These influences generally can be classified as the faddish academics with whom one associates and works in the musty Halls of the Academy. Such colleagues—who might be called "radical-chic" if they had the money to throw big parties for César Chávez—provided the prototypes for the Anglo as that term is used in this work. They saved me many long hours of research into the Anglo makeup, for they served as perfect models for the Puritanical intolerance that has become the hallmark of the bleeding heart liberal.

Finally, there should be some attempt at definition. Unfortunately, I, too, used a stereotypic word throughout the work. Anglo as used here refers to modern day Puritans, those believers in homogeneity and conformity to an established set of *mores* who in their apostolic fanaticism deny individuality and true pluralism in our melting-pot society. Certainly the mass of people of varying ethnic stocks in our country do not fit such a characterization. But they generally have little clout among opinion makers who inundate them with pernicious nonsense. For me the Anglo as defined is an advocate of "group think" and conformity; he is not a believer in individualism except for himself and his cohorts. Therefore, these must also be thanked for their contribution.

All of the influences—positive and negative—and all of the help I received in this work do not absolve the author from final responsibility. I gladly shoulder it.

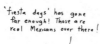

Part I

Legacies in Conflict

When Anglos first began trickling into Spanish and then Mexican territory over the Santa Fe Trail and on sailing vessels that reached the coast of California, they encountered a civilization already fully developed. The way of life encountered by enterprising Anglos when they first reached the new territories both shocked and enchanted the first Yankee settlers of the Southwest and California. The Yankees found a culture predicated upon an aristocratic principle that was Roman Catholic and Hispanic; the social traditions, the economic practices, and the religion of the Hispanic inhabitants ran counter to the principles upon which the fledgling United States was founded.

At the same time the initial intrusions of Yankee traders and trappers into Spanish and Mexican territories failed to posit a clear and present threat to the Hispano inhabitants. To them, the North Americans presented a ready market for some of the agricultural and pastoral products produced in Arizona, New Mexico, Texas, and California. After 1821, when Mexico achieved her independence from Spain, the flow of Yankees into Mexican territory, combined with United States intrusions in Mexican politics, emerged as a positive danger to the hegemony of Mexican culture and territorial sovereignty.

Cultural differences between Anglos and Hispanos readily manifested themselves as members of both groups came into close proximity. The patterns of culture bequeathed to both Hispano and Anglo were formulated in the sixteenth century and ingrained themselves to produce the potential for conflict that presently polarizes both groups.

The arrival of Spain in the New World was presaged by a long, grueling 811-year battle against the Moorish invaders of the Iberian peninsula. In 1492, Queen Isabella of Castile gave her grant to Christopher Columbus to explore the lands to the West in an attempt to find a western route to Cathay. Until that year, Spain was too involved to join in the overseas competition with Portugal. The ouster of the Moors in 1492, however, presented Castile with an opportunity to join the maritime race. Instead of Cathay, of course, Columbus found the Indies and thereby set the stage for subsequent Spanish expansion first into the Caribbean and then on to the mainland of North and South America.

In 1517, one expedition landed off of Mexico's southern coast. The following year another expedition made contact again in the south. By 1519, Diego de Velázquez, the Spanish Governor of Cuba, selected young Hernán Cortés to head an expedition to what would become Mexico or the Viceroyalty of New Spain.

Cortés typified the Spanish gentleman of the early sixteenth century. Like so many of his class and generation, Cortés was a product of medieval religiosity and the cold hearted secularism of a Machiavellian Renaissance. The Spaniards of the early conquest period in the New World came with a zeal for propagating the Faith, aggrandizing themselves, and achieving a personal glory that would have been unattainable if they had remained in Spain. Cortés and his contemporaries carried with them a tradition of battling for a religious principle that, in many respects, would be attacked from all quarters after the Lutheran Reformation of 1517.

In a social sense, the Spanish adventurers typified by Cortés were reared on an aristocratic premise. It was expected that the wellborn would achieve glory either in arms or in the Church. As a result, the discovery and subsequent colonization of the New World offered outlets for the lesser nobility of Spain to make their way and achieve what was expected of people in their station. Battling against the Moorish invaders implanted in the Spaniards a religious and social militancy that ultimately carried over into the New World.

The Spaniards in the New World represented a highly centralized nation ready to expand territorially and politically. Spain, moreover, became the defender of a Faith threatened by Protestant schism and international beleaguering throughout the sixteenth century. Discovery of precious metals in many parts of her American empire engendered international rivalry which, in turn, was heightened by the religious rivalry touched off by a questioning monk at Wittenburg in 1517.

It was, therefore, with a sense of pride in himself and in the Crown of Castile that Cortés left Cuba in February, 1519, to consummate the expedition to the mainland of Mexico. He first landed in Tabasco and then proceeded to Veracruz later in the Spring. At both places contact was made with the Indian inhabitants, and it was at Tabasco that Cortés made his first major find, a woman.

She was an Aztec princess captured by the Maya in one of

their interminable feuds with the Aztecs. Her name became Doña Marina, and, according to Salvador de Madariaga, she fascinated Cortés far more than did his wife in Cuba. She proved invaluable to Cortés, for she became infatuated with the blond, bearded conquistador and served him as interpreter, spy, and mistress. It was this physical as well as cultural union of Cortés and Marina that ultimately epitomized the fusion of cultures that would occur in Mexico after the long bloody conquest and the arduous process of colonization.

The Amerindian civilization found in Mexico at the time of the Spanish Conquest was already in a state of decay. In Yucatán, the Maya had undergone cyclical periods of ascendancy and decline characterized by high degrees of governmental centralization and achievements in science and the arts. In 1519, the Maya were decentralized and therefore more susceptible to conquest. In the valley of Mexico, the Nahua-speaking groups fought each other for prominence until the Mexica (pronounced Mesheeca) tribe became the most powerful element and forged the Aztec empire throughout the fifteenth century. Yet, by 1519, the massive empire began to show signs of ultimate collapse. Imperial expansion by the Mexica broadened their influence throughout the valley of Mexico, enhanced the glory of the Emperor at Tenochtitlán, and alienated other Nahua-speaking tribes in the perimeter of the empire.

Added to the expansionist tendencies among the Mexica was a problem in Aztec theology. The principal diety of the Mexica was a little hummingbird with the incredible name of Huitzilopochtli. This ravenous little bird possessed an insatiable thirst for human blood, and his little belly craved human cardiac tissue. To keep the little beasty happy and to assure Aztec successes the priests of the temple at Tenochtitlán showered him with human sacrifices. Thus, tribute from subject tribes was often demanded in human flesh in order to satisfy the gods. The ever increasing demand for tribute, in turn, caused the subject tribes to become restless under Aztec dominance, and they looked to the return of Quetzalcoatl, a benign member of the Pantheon, to deliver them from oppression.

Quetzalcoatl was represented by a feathered serpent and had been the principal diety of the Toltecs, former inhabitants of Teotihuacan. When the Mexica arrived in the valley of Mexico and established Tenochtitlán they began their expansionism toward Teotihuacán. With the elevation of Huitzilopochtli, Quetzalcoatl retreated to his home in the East to return as a white man with a hairy face. (Have patience, I'm almost through with these Nahuatl names.)

The arrival of Cortés at Veracruz gave the Aztec emperor, Montezuma II, cause for remorse. Could the Quetzalcoatl legend be true? Was that white, bearded man really the feathered serpent coming back to deliver his oppressed people? God knows, the time was right. According to legend, Mr. Q. had promised to return in the Aztec equivalent of 1519. Montezuma set ambushes, but these failed to stop the mysterious white men progressing slowly from the East. The Spaniards, through a delicate web of diplomacy between themselves and tribes who held an enmity toward the Aztecs, relentlessly pushed on toward Tenochtitlán. Gifts of gold, precious stones, and quetzal feathers failed to appease Cortés and his rugged crew. They pushed on, destroying pagan temples, baptizing Indians (and especially the women with whom they bedded), and searching for riches that were promised as a result of participation in the venture.

It required three years for Cortés to bring the Aztecs under control. Internal dissension, conflict with a rival expedition from Cuba, plus rebellion by the Indians made the Conquest less neat than Cortés wished. Yet, the final upshot of the Conquest was the intricate diplomatic ties that Cortés used to achieve his ends. Force was the final and most desperate alternative. Diplomacy should be tried first. In this Cortés showed

himself a consummate genius. His alliance with the Tlaxcalte-
cos carried over into the period of colonization and served
Spain well in her expansion into northern Mexico and the
Southwest.

The consummation of the Conquest of Mexico allowed
the Spanish imperial powers to transplant Castilian institutions in what Cortés named New Spain. At the urging of
Hernán Cortés the Castilian crown sent to Mexico missionary
fathers for the conversion of the Indians and the extirpation of
heathenism. The process of conversion which the first Franciscans brought to Mexico not only included religious instruction but also an attempt to Hispanicize the Indian. In 1523, for
example, the Fleming Franciscan, Peter of Ghent or Pedro de
Gante, established a school for the sons of Indian nobility in
order to facilitate Hispanization.

Dedicated missionaries carried out religious instruction in
the sixteenth century. They learned the Indian languages and
adapted Indian religious practices where they were com-
patible with Catholicism. For example, the Indians viewed
baptism as sacramental, and this neatly dovetailed into the
Christian scheme. Auricular confession was another parallel.
Most striking, from the indigenous point of view, was the existence of saints in the Christian theology. To the Indian, the
saints represented gods unto themselves that closely resembled
the deposed Nahua dieties.

The most significant religious phenomenon to occur in
Mexico was the apparation of the Virgin of Guadalupe on
December 12, 1531. Here the cynics can have a holiday. On
December 9, 1531, an apparition appeared to an Indian boy
named Juan Diego. He was told to go to the hill of Tepeyac
and gather roses. Juan Diego, not a particularly bright lad,
knew enough, however, to discern that there were absolutely
no roses on the hill of Tepeyac. Any bloody fool should know
that only prickly pear cactuses or nopales grew there. As the
story goes, he went to see the Bishop of Mexico, Fray Juan de
Zumárraga. Zumárraga told the boy to obey the vision. Thus,

on December 12, off went Juan Diego to Tepeyac. Lo and be-
hold, there were the roses. He gathered them into his cloak and
heeled and toed it back to Mexico City to show them to the
Bishop. When he arrived, he opened his cloak and instead of
roses he found an imprint of the Virgin Mary. What is striking
about this particular phenomenon is that the Virgin appeared
to an Indian boy, she was brown skinned and black haired,
and, to make the coincidence more telling, she appeared upon
the Tepeyac, the hill that once held the Temple of Tonántzin,
the Indian Virgin Mother. Wags can scoff at this and say that
Zumárraga found a highly impressionable patsy to help facilitate conversion. Perhaps he did. But what is incontrovertible is
the fact that the process of conversion accelerated with the appearance of an Indian Virgin. Moreover, the supposedly
original cloak that belonged to Juan Diego has defied scientific
analysis, for the dyes that made the impression have never been
broken down.

As New Spain moved out of Tenochtitlán or Mexico City
and made inroads into the frontier regions, Spanish institutions followed. Next to religion the significant parallel between Spaniard and Indian was social organization. Both were
aristocratic in structure. When the Spaniards arrived in New
Spain, they made alliances with Indian nobility, married the
daughters of Indian caciques ("chieftains"), and the indigenous nobles received the same privileges as Spanish gentlemen. As a result, overlapping social organizations made social
mobility more fluid. Social distinction depended, ultimately,
less on race than one's place on a fluid social ladder. Both
cultures were predicated upon a laboring mass. The Spaniards
brought with them the *encomienda* system for both Christian-
izing the Indians and at the same time providing for labor for
mines and fields.

Protection of the Indian from exploitation became a paramount consideration of the Spanish Crown. Legislation from
the Council of the Indies ringed the *encomenderos* (holders of
encomiendas) with restrictions. The most important corpus of

legislation was the New Laws of 1542. Yet, the reception of this legislation in New Spain was so hostile that the Viceroy, Antonio de Mendoza, forced modifications in the law.

Instrumental in the passage of the New Laws was a Dominican friar, the Bishop of Chiapas, Bartolomé de las Casas. Las Casas came to the New World before the conquest of Mexico. While on the Isle of Hispaniola he repented holding Indians in *encomienda* and began a lifelong campaign to relieve the Indians of the burdens imposed upon them by the Spanish conquerors. He badgered the Crown so much that Charles V finally gave him the title of Protector of the Indians. A problem, however, arose; Las Casas took the title seriously. Tracts and harangues poured from the pen of the hardy Dominican. He wrote voluminously and lobbied with the vigor of oil companies trying to maintain a depletion allowance. His major works, including a *History of the Destruction of the Indies,* painted the Spanish conquerors and colonizers as uniquely cruel individuals intent upon the pure exploitation of the Indian subjects. What right did Spain have to exploit these childlike creatures, declared Las Casas? Crown theologians responded that Spain's whole function was to convert the Indians because, according to the Papal Grant of 1493, Castile could not occupy the lands in the West unless she did so with the intention of propagating the Faith.

Generally, however, minds more sane than Las Casas prevailed. Eminent jurists like the Jesuit Francisco de Victoria argued that war against the heathen was allowable under certain conditions. Imperial and religious policy blended into a justification for conversion of the Indian and for his exploitation as labor. Again, however, Indian labor was ringed by legalistic restrictions. Often these were observed in the breach more than in the practice, but the principle of Indian protection became the paramount cornerstone of Spanish policy in the New World.

From Mexico-Tenochtitlán Spain spread her control to

the north, south, east, and west. Silver mines were discovered in Zacatecas in 1546 and with the growth of mining in northern Mexico the hacienda, or large land holding, came into its own.

In the northern provinces of New Spain the hacienda became the major social unit. The *hacendado* (owner) ran a self-sufficient operation. Mestizo (mixed bloods) and Indian laborers lived, procreated, and died on the hacienda. What was developed was an intimate personal relationship between *hacendado* and *peón*. Called the *patrón-peón* relationship by the more scholarly, this symbolized a unit of social organization that would be transferred to the Southwest and California. Personal relationships were established between the boss and his hired hands. Often the *peones* asked the *hacendados* to act as godparents for their children. Such a union drew all elements closer together. In an aristocratic system, there was no thought of equality. It is only in the twentieth century that the hacienda became the monster of human exploitation. From all accounts, and admittedly the evidence is still sketchy, things worked fairly well on the large haciendas of northern Mexico and the Southwest.

Thus, Spain arrived at 1600 with her Mexican imperial appendage established and thriving. Mining, cattle raising, commerce, and home industries characterized her economy. More significantly, however, was the establishment of a social and economic system on the haciendas that ultimately allowed for a modicum of self government and that established a pattern for relations between the *patrón-peón* initially and then between political bosses and their followers. This, however, became more important after Mexico achieved her independence, after the Southwest, Texas, and California became a part of the United States, and during this century.

While Spain climbed the trail of imperial glory in the sixteenth century, the rest of Europe indulged in carping about

Spanish expansionism while at the same time happily accepting the bullion used by Spain for the purchase of merchandise in other European countries. Spain suffered the dilemma of being top dog on the European totem pole. Her lessers complained incessantly about Spain's imperial successes both on the Continent and in the New World and constantly intrigued for a piece of the action.

Another problem persisted to plague Spain as well, especially after 1517. Religious schism ruptured the idea of universal Christendom. Spain emerged as the embattled defender of a Catholic orthodoxy that, after the mid-sixteenth century, fused with political and diplomatic problems.

Countering Spain was England. Henry VIII's monomaniacal desire to sire a male heir for the throne of England forced him to break with the Church of Rome in order to legitimize his wife-swapping. The English break with the Holy See exacerbated the enmity between Spain and England. To the Spaniards, England was schismatic, forcing the faithful dwelling within her frontiers to observe invalid religious practices. As if this were not bad enough, English corsairs already plagued the bullion shipments coming from the New World to Castile.

Reformation and Counterreformation set the tone for the struggle between Iberian and English cultures. Spain's enemies, spearheaded by the English and the secessionist Dutch in the late sixteenth century, found an abundance of evidence to use against Spain in the war for men's souls and for Spanish territory. Much of the evidence cited by the English and the Dutch about the unique perversion of the Spaniards was supplied by Spaniards themselves. Las Casas' works gave Spain's enemies first hand testimony about the rapacity and greed that characterized Spain's representatives in the New World. Such a cacophony of acrimony aimed at the Spanish inculcated in the English an intense dislike for anything Iberian, including religion, complexion, language, and general culture.

Another factor worked against Spain in the eyes of her European competitors. She had the much maligned Inquisition. That handy institution strove to maintain religious orthodoxy in a country whose unifying principle was Catholicism. The Holy Office both in Spain and in her New World Empire diligently ferreted out heretics and apostates. Moreover, the Inquisitors worked industriously to clean the Church from within. Heretical clerics and licentious priests who violated the sanctity of the confessional came under Inquisitorial purview. Unfortunately, some English sailors were occasionally processed in a country that rejected schism and the result was an increased enmity toward Spain.

England earnestly joined the imperial race in the early seventeenth century. At the same time internal difficulties plagued the country as increasing dissension threatened to rip her apart in the first half of the century. Nearly a century had elapsed since the publication of Las Casas' works on the Indies, the Reformation and Counterreformation overworked the printing presses in propaganda production, and cultural patterns had been well established by the time Oliver Cromwell came to power in England at mid-century.

English colonial activity moved to North America. The founding of Plymouth, Jamestown, and other colonies on the Atlantic seaboard introduced into the Americas a colonial transplant of English attitudes vis-à-vis Spain and her imperial appendages.

Paramount among the English attitudes transplanted in the New World was a loathing for Catholicism. With the exception of Maryland, a colony founded by the Catholic Lord Baltimore, most of the other colonies took a dim if not completely intolerant view toward things that smacked of Popery. Thus, England's imperial competition with Spain received additional impetus from an increasingly ingrained bias against obscurantist Catholicism represented by the Iberian monarchs.

Southern planters in Maryland, Virginia, and the

Carolinas took a more tolerant view of Catholics, but New England, stronghold of Puritan divines, became the hotbed of Calvinism in North America. The Calvinists brought to America the dreary notion that industriousness and diligence might indicate election to that happy place in the sky. In so doing, American Puritans have been characterized as pinch-faced tightwads who opposed anything that might indicate an unseemly display of fun. Apparently some scholarly studies demonstrated that this was not the case. But, it should be noted, most of the United States scholarly community is composed of latter-day Puritans anyway. Be that as it may, the doctrine of hard work and individual accomplishment in the economic realm became a sacrosanct principle in North America. One's place in society was attained through labor and not by initial social class. This proved to be a fine theory but failed to work out that way in practice.

Thus, diametrically opposed social and economic systems faced each other in North America. In Spanish North America, Roman Catholicism and Hispanic culture held sway while on the Atlantic Seaboard English religion and English life style was the rule. Polarity existed. Ultimately, this polarization of attitudes would be felt as Yankees pushed westward and collided with Spaniards and Mexicans.

A factor that most distinguished the English from the Spanish-Mexican colonists was the respective attitudes toward the indigenous inhabitants of the area. The English attitude was simple and expedient: push the filthy savages back into the hinterlands or annihilate them. English colonists in North America came to the New World, in part, not to propagate a universal faith but to maintain a schismatic one. The idea of mingling with the heathen, despite the good offices of Poca-hontas and the friendly bunch at Plymouth, was anathema to the English. For one thing, they looked different. Where were the pasty complexions and drawn faces so necessary for a proper appearance? The English experience with people of color was negligible. To the English the thought of intimate contact with the Amerindians seemed repugnant. It should be noted also that this same repugnance carried over to intimate physical contact with Negro slaves. Yet, the incidence of mulatto children on plantations in the United States certainly indicates the triumph of libido over physical revulsion.

Spaniards and subsequently Mexicans felt no compunction about contact with Indians and Blacks. While racial prejudice did exist, the overall tenor of colonial Mexican society was one of permissiveness in relations between the races. Early in the Spanish colonial experience the conquistadores were encouraged to marry Indian women and thereby accelerate the process of assimilation of the indigenous people.

The majority of unions between Indian and Spaniard were not sacramental. Rather, Indian women became the mistresses of Spaniards and Creoles who maintained a *casa chica*. The *casa chica*, or little house, proved a convenience for Creole and Spanish men who were enamored with a mistress but were unfortunately tied to a very proper wife. Children emanating from this union were called mestizos or halfbreeds, and created yet another class in the social hierarchy of New Spain. One scholar of colonial Mexico attributes the ultimate triumph of Spain to the *membrum febriles* rather than either sword or cross. The Indian women readily gave themselves to the conquistadores and, as a result, produced the mestizos that comprise 80 percent of Mexico's population today.

The mestizo hung suspended between two cultures. Usually coming from an Indian mother, he became schizophrenic about whether he was Indian or Spanish. In point of fact, it made little difference in the long run. Amalgamation of blood reached such a point by the end of the eighteenth century that the racial distinctions had social rather than racial meanings. Thus, an *indio*, or Indian, did not necessarily have to be an Indian by blood. Rather his life style more closely approached that of the indigenous peoples than that of the Spanish.

Crown encouragement of miscegenation proved a valuable asset in the ultimate conquest and colonization of New Spain. For one thing, it became easier to incorporate the Indian nobility into the Spanish hierarchy if familial ties existed. Indian nobles obtained the same prequisites as Spanish and later Creole gentlemen. They could bear arms, they could ride horses, they could wear cloaks that denoted them as gentlemen, and the Indian nobility were eager to be accepted by their Spanish conquerors.

The process of Indian incorporation resulted in much Indian assistance in Spanish expansion into northern Mexico and the Southwest. Tlaxcaltecos and Otomies became spearheads of Spanish expansion in the North. The city of Saltillo, for example, was settled largely by Tlaxcaltecos. These enjoyed a unique position in Spanish favor. They had originally treated with Cortés in an alliance that ultimately brought down the worshippers of Huitzilopochtli and were therefore given a number of immunities and favors by the Spanish crown. Their cooperation in the northward expansion of New Spain was testimony to the acceptance of the Spaniards by the Indians.

By 1700, the cultural attitudes of English and Spanish-Mexicans vis-à-vis each other and their relative positions in the New World were reasonable established. Spain and England continued in their conflict, though by 1700 the ostensible religious motive diminished considerably. Anglo and Hispano would continue to butt heads in North America. Spanish moves north of the Rio Grande were often strategic. Underlying all of the territorial maneuvering was an implicit dislike for each other's cultural patterns. In Spanish North America a cultural system was continued and expanded into the borderlands.

2

Cultures at Loggerheads

Every August at the full moon Santa Barbara, California, indulges in an orgy of "love your friendly greaser." Referred to more politely as Fiesta or Old Spanish Days, the Santa Barbarians retreat back to a romanticized past when caballeros on spirited horseflesh pranced about and demure señoritas clad in mantillas and waving seductively with lace fans dominated the California scene. Old Spanish Days is but one of many examples of the dominant Anglo culture in California and the Southwest attempting to relive the thing that it destroyed when half of Mexico's territory was ceded to the United States in 1848. Yet, in typical Anglo fashion, the thing only lasts for

about a week because too long a contact with "greaser" culture might contaminate the dominant Anglo. Old Spanish
days emerges, then, as yet another sop to the idea of California's Spanish and Mexican past. The late summer phenomenon fails, however, to come to grips with historical reality and
with the incontrovertible fact that Anglo culture ultimately
shunted aside a fully developed civilization and replaced it
with its own peculiar life style. Yet, the Anglo drags out the
Mexican once a year in an attempt to assuage a nagging conscience through some phony recognition of the halcyon days of
the Rancheros.

The impasse in which the Anglo finds himself contains
deep historical roots dating back to the early Spanish settlement of the Southwest and California. Direct, permanent penetration of the Southwest began in 1598 when Juan de Oñate led
an expedition into New Mexico. The Oñate expedition was
but one attempt, this time successful, to establish Spanish
hegemony beyond the borders of Spain's northern mining
frontier. The Spanish settlement of New Mexico brought into
direct contact Spaniards and Indians once again. As in the
previous conquest of central Mexico, military forces were used
only as an expediency. What became paramount in Spanish
maneuvering in New Mexico was the close relationship that
developed between the Indian and the Spaniard. Of course,
Indian resistance received harsh treatment from Spanish forces,
and for eighty years the conquered Indians nursed animosities
against the Spaniards. Long-standing Indian displeasure over
the new arrangement in New Mexico resulted in the Pueblo
Revolt of 1680. At the same time, it arose from maladministra-
tion and a nearly studied neglect of New Mexico by the
Spanish imperial authorities. New Mexico produced no precious metals, and, while there were souls to be saved, was it
worth redeeming the heathen if there were no material return
in this world?

Despite the neglect by Spain of her province to the far
north, settlers from Mexico came in after Oñate and his band

consummated the initial pacification. As in other parts of
Spain's vast Mexican empire, Spanish colonists began mingling almost immediately with the Indian women. More
mestizos were born as a result of the initial hanky-panky between conqueror and conquered. By the time of the Pueblo
revolt, the distinctions between Spaniard and mestizo became
less noticeable and both ultimately blended into the generic
classification of Hispano as opposed to the purely indigenous.

On another front was the attempt to reach California.
This effort began as early as 1535 when Hernán Cortés sent an
expedition to find the passage to Cathay. Of course, what was
discovered was Baja California, believed to be an island by the
Spanish conquerors, but efforts from Cortés until the late
seventeenth century proved fruitless. Ultimately, what prepared the way for the final Spanish thrust into California was
the pacification of Arizona and northern Baja California.

Leading the Spanish move into Sonora and what is now
Arizona was an indefatigable Jesuit by the name of Eusebio
Kino, a German from the Tyrol who specialized in mathe-
matics. Father Kino, however, felt the call to missionary work
and asked for transfer to the mission field. A ready area opened
up as he arrived in Mexico in the 1680's. Sonora with her
Apache-like tribes needed to be brought under Spanish control. Until his death in 1711, Kino worked the mission field of
Sonora and Arizona. He often traveled alone or accompanied
by one or two Indians. Kino moved into southern Arizona and
other Jesuit fathers under his supervision carried sacraments
and holy writ to the heathen of Baja California. When Kino
died in 1711, the stage was set for Spanish strategic moves into
California.

Yet, Spain was distracted from her imperial activities in
1700. She was left without an heir to the throne. The last Hapsburg, the undeniably idiotic Charles II, refused to die until
1700. Everything was tried to bring about procreation. Aphro-
disiacs failed, enticing women failed to arouse the demented
Charles, and, ultimately, exorcism of the devil by a most

energetic monk did not produce a Hapsburg heir to the Spanish throne. As a result, Charles, in a flash of lucidity, willed the throne to the nearest candidate, the grandson of Louis XIV of France, Philip, the Duke of Anjou. Austria's Hapsburgs also held a claim to the throne. The conflicting claims precipitated a war between France and practically everybody else. France lost the war militarily but won the throne of Spain for Philip who became Philip V. England, who was pitted against France in the encounter, gained some minor trade concessions but these merely recognized tacitly the smuggling that England had been doing in the Spanish colonies for a century.

Of greater import for the borderlands area were the administrative reforms that accompanied Bourbon rule of Spain and her American empire. The Bourbon kings of Spain from Philip V onward brought with them techniques tried and proven workable in France. Efficiency characterized the Bourbon administration of New Spain. It should be noted, however, that this efficiency was purely a comparative matter, for the Bourbons encountered some terrible logjams but at the same time were able to resolve them more expeditiously than their Hapsburg predecessors.

With the Bourbon kings of Spain, the empire received a greater emphasis on a functioning bureaucracy predicated on merit and experience. Thus, when offices were created for New Spain, they were filled with men who had the necessary noble requisites but were also endowed with the administrative experience necessary for the management of a far-flung empire. In Spain old traditional practices passed away and the cult of efficiency replaced them. With this came advancement of individuals within the bureaucratic framework on the basis of merit and performance rather than purely on social connections.

Spain's Bourbon monarchs strove to rationalize the administration of the colonies. New Spain, as it had expanded for two centuries, was becoming increasingly unwieldy. Strategic moves forced Spain in the early eighteenth century to expand into Texas and Louisiana in an attempt to stem the pressures from both England and France. In addition, marauding Indians constantly threatened Spanish presidios and villages in the areas of New Mexico, Arizona, and Texas. Thus, the efficiency-minded Charles III, after preliminary investigations, created the *Provincias Internas* out of the provinces of New Mexico, Chihuahua, Coahuila, and Texas and made them nearly autonomous units.

In the *Provincias Internas* a less rigid social system evolved. Indians, for example, were not held in *encomienda* even in New Mexico. The system outlived its usefulness by 1600 and so was not established in New Mexico during the Oñate expedition. Moreover, the major colonizers and administrators in the *Provincias Internas* were of a different breed. Bourbon rationalism replaced the more religiously orthodox Hapsburgs. As a result, the Age of Enlightenment manifested itself on the borderlands through the establishment of efficient administrative units that were often devoid of humanity but did produce more pesos for the empire.

The Spanish move into California proved a strategic response to Russian intrusions into northern California. Because of the relationship between French and Spanish Bourbons, Spain found herself dragged into that long series of wars between France and England that finally resolved themselves with the Seven Years' War, or the French and Indian War (1754-1763). From this caper Spain gained a piece of Louisiana, and, to her good luck, had France removed from her northeastern back. But the damned Russians persisted. Thus, in the 1770's an expedition headed by Gaspar de Portolá crossed the desert from Sonora to California and began founding villages. The first was present-day San Diego, California. Of especial import for this expedition was the continued presence of missionary clergy. This time Franciscans, headed by

Fray Junípero Serra, led the clerical contingent. The Jesuits were expelled from Spain's empire in 1767, victims of misguided rationalism.

From San Diego northward to Monterey, Father Serra and his Franciscans worked at the Christianization of the heathen. Missions were founded and villages were built. Once work among the heathen stabilized, Serra and some of his coreligionists pushed on to continue God's work. At the same time more settlers moved into California, establishing ranches on the lines of the haciendas of the *Provincias Internas*.

A social system predicated primarily on a pastoral society emerged in both the *Provincias Internas* and in California. The Spanish settlers of the area prided themselves on their Spanish heritage and, by 1800, disliked being classified as Mexicans though in point of fact very few of the settlers were from Spain. The social system was aristocratic. Land not only measured wealth but also prestige. Manual labor belonged to the menial classes, both Indian and mestizos, and the Hispanos felt no compunction about indulging in hedonist whirls of fiestas, bullfights, and bear baiting. It became apparent that the Protestant work ethic would ultimately clash when the two cultures came together.

Yet, revolutionary ferment throughout the Western World in the latter part of the eighteenth century would affect profoundly the situation in the borderlands. The first major revolution of the eighteenth century occurred in England's North American colonies between 1776 and 1783. Bellowing such earthy slogans as "No taxation without representation," the colonists indulged themselves in a fit of throwing the lobster-backed bastards out of North America. To be sure, the American Revolution had justification, for England for too long had neglected her overseas colonies. Only after 1763 did the English begin to act like an imperial power. But then it was too late. The colonies, neglected by the mother country throughout most of the seventeenth and eighteenth centuries, fended for themselves and were by now accustomed to managing their own affairs. As a result, English pressures forced the revolution that ultimately created the United States.

Underlying much of the American Revolution was the cultural inspiration emanating from Europe. The intoxicating theories of Montesquieu and the other eighteenth century philosophes implanted in the North Americans the ideas of juridical equality, of representative govenment, of checks and balances. At the same time, the North Americans ended up believing that their unique system would ultimately be the salvation of the Western Hemisphere. The embodiment of these ideas in the United States Constitution became an inspiration ultimately for the Mexicans and the inhabitants of the borderlands.

Revolution, however, continued to spread. This time, France became the focal point of ferment. In 1789, a massive revolution was unleashed that overthrew the Old Regime and produced a heady array of propaganda for a new social order. Since the United States successfully ousted a monarch, logically the French could do the same thing. In this they proved eminently successful except for one thing. Not only did they oust poor Louis XVI, they also beheaded the poor slob.

France's revolution, because of the intensity of its impact, brought about a reaction against Jacobin radicalism and ushered in an era of short-lived Imperial glory. When Napoleon Bonaparte took power in 1799, the stage was set. Napoleon proceeded to war on France's enemies and neighbors in an attempt to aggrandize himself and France. He pushed into the Germanies and into the Iberian peninsula. In 1807-1808, French troops pushed into Spain and Portugal, deposed the existing monarchies, and established French puppets on the Iberian thrones. The effects of this seizure would, ultimately, have a telling effect upon the reactions of the Mexicans and upon the borderlands areas that were the northern appendages of Spain's North American empire.

Inevitably, the revolutionary ferment that touched the United States and France reached the Spanish borderlands in

North America. Even before France erupted in bloody revolt, United States citizens made casual intrusions into Louisiana and into east Texas. By 1800 with France in the Napoleonic grip and with Spain precariously balancing between war and neutrality with France, the Spanish borderlands experienced a greater influx of gringos into the area. One such gringo, an Irishman named Philip Nolan, led a band into Texas. Spanish authorities surprised Nolan's filibustering expedition, killed, Nolan, and took the captives to Chihuahua. Such an event apprised Spain of early expansionist tendencies by the recently created United States, for Spain believed that Nolan and his crew were intent on capturing Texas and Northern Mexico for the new nation east of the Mississippi.

Two other events between 1800 and the Napoleonic invasion of the Iberian peninsula in 1807 caused the Spanish borderlands considerable apprehension. The first of these was the French cession of the Louisiana Territory to the United States in 1803. This placed the already suspect gringos in very close proximity to New Spain and threatened to bring about a greater influx of Anglos from the United States into Mexico. The second thing was the Aaron Burr conspiracy of 1806. Apparently, Burr and his conspiratorial crew hoped to acquire a considerable chunk of Northern Mexico and form an independent republic with Burr as its head. The conspiracy was broken, but the Spanish and Mexican authorities came to a greater realization of the expansionist milieu that characterized the United States.

But the Napoleonic invasion of Spain touched off a series of events that finally led to Mexican independence. A Mexican nationalism, originally flaccid before 1808, erupted in 1810 when a parish priest, Father Miguel Hidalgo y Costilla, issued the *Grito de Dolores* on September 16 that led to Mexican independence in 1821. The causes for Mexican independence lay in the social system that was erected by the Spanish imperial powers. Top positions went to the *peninsulares,* or Spaniards born in Spain, rather than to Creoles, or Spaniards born in the New World. Hidalgo and other Creoles felt the snub intensely. Reared on Voltaire, Montesquieu, and Rousseau, Hidalgo could not see why he was relegated to a backwoods parish instead of being given a more prominent position within the Church. Some man of God, this one!

News of revolt in Mexico proper spread rather quickly. Though Hidalgo was captured, processed by the Inquisition, and executed in less than a year after the beginning of the near race riot that passed for an independence movement, the ferment for independence continued. In Texas, for example, a filibustering expedition led by some of Hidalgo's former followers moved against the Gulf coast in 1813. They succeeded in forcing a Spanish retreat and brought about the surrender of San Antonio. Both Mexicans and Americans fled to the United States from Texas, and the United States government, realizing that Spain was still a friendly power, warned against any involvement in the difficulties with Spain. Yet, Spain saw the aggressive gringos as a potential threat, for in east Texas they could establish cotton plantations and extend their commercial and agricultural activities. Private American involvement continued in Texas, though it received no official sanction from the United States.

In New Mexico, the opening of the Louisiana Territory brought greater American commercial activity into the area. By 1810, the Americans were no longer curiosities around Santa Fe, for they began trading in the region as early as 1806. New Mexico, however, was relieved of some of the revolutionary tensions that broke out throughout New Spain after 1810.

California felt but little the impact of the independence movement. It was not until after Hidalgo and his successors were successfully out of the picture that the ripples of independence made themselves felt there. This does not say, however, that California was isolated, for before 1800 foreigners were already interested in the area. British, Italian, and French visitors came to California, and by 1796, an American vessel was in Monterey Harbor. Foreign interest in this far-flung portion of Spain's deteriorating empire was manifest.

Yet, by 1820, all of Spain's empire was going by the boards. Many of the South American countries were free from Spanish control. Mexico, by 1821, would be fully independent. Surprisingly, Mexican independence was characterized ultimately not by a liberal movement but by a conservative one that enthroned the Creole Agustín de Iturbide as Agustín I of the Mexican Empire. Developments in Spain proved too liberal for the generally conservative Mexican Creoles. With independence came concomitant chaos that ultimately resulted in greater United States penetration of former Spanish territory and an eruption of cultural conflict.

Mexico independence introduced a plethora of problems for the borderlands region. The establishment of some form of government required that the rebel leaders in Mexico City dedicate themselves to the long, difficult process of rendering into writing the basis of government. Initially, Mexico began her independent status as an empire, but by 1823, liberal forces, goaded on by Joel R. Poinsett, on a special mission to Mexico, overthrew the Iturbide regime and began working on a constitution.

Poinsett, as United States minister to Mexico, became instrumental in supporting the liberal Constitution of 1824. In form, at least, the new Constitution resembled that of the United States. Yet, the process of drawing up the document revealed severe schisms within the Mexican body politic. On the one hand there were the Centralists who believed that the best solution to the problems of the fledgling Mexican nation rested in a strong central authority that possessed the ultimate authority in national and state affairs. On the other hand, the Federalists (not to be confused with those in the United States) were states' rights advocates. The Constitution of 1824 showed a preponderance of Federalism. This initial Federalist influence spelled a death knell for constitutionalism in Mexico, for the forces released during the struggle for independence continued and ripped the fabric of the Mexican political garment.

Despite the copying of constitutional forms from the United States, the newly independent Mexican government viewed suspiciously the activities of the United States and its citizens in its northern territories. Spain's experience with Yankee traders before Mexican independence indicated the particularly chauvinistic nature of the Anglo-American. Even before Spain surrendered Mexico, Moses Austin bickered with Spanish authorities for permission to bring colonists from Tennessee and Kentucky into east Texas.

Austin's health, however, failed him, and his son, Stephen F. Austin ended up bringing the expedition into Texas. Texas, at one time a part of the former *Provincias Internas,* was sparsely populated, and Spanish and later Mexican authorities proved reticent about allowing the flow of Americans to increase into that area. Yet, they granted permission to Austin to go to Texas.

By 1830 internal difficulties in Mexico and in Texas proper heightened the tension between Anglos and Mexicans in the area. In Mexico the political situation continued chaotic with vast swings of the political pendulum from Centralist to Federalist. In 1830 Antonio López de Santa Anna, Mexico's perennial political chameleon, was in power, saw the threat of increased gringo entry into Texas, and took measures to stem the flow. He approached the Texas problem from two angles: first, Santa Anna's Congress joined Texas to the State of Coahuila to make it a single administrative unit and thus give Mexicans a preponderance in the state legislature. Secondly, slavery was abolished in Mexico in an attempt to undercut the Americans flowing into the cotton areas of east Texas.

Protests arose in Texas proper with both resident

Mexicans and Anglos complaining about the usurpation of state integrity by the Central Government. Yet, the Texans, both Anglo and Mexican, remained loyal to the Mexican Government, for conditions were bound to change in Mexico's kaleidoscope political milieu. In point of fact, the situation did change. Liberals overthrew Santa Anna's puppet, and installed a new regime headed, of course, by the indomitable Santa Anna and his vice president, the liberal Valentín Gómez Farías. Such action mollified the Texans, but their relief was shortlived. In 1834, thirteen months after the liberal government had been installed, Santa Anna emerged as the defender of privilege and religion and led the attack against the liberals.

Liberal constitutional principles were ignored by the ruling conservative group. A supreme power was installed as a watchdog committee to rule the nation, and this, ultimately, proved too much for the Texans. Sam Houston and a band of angry Texans and liberal Mexicans pronounced against the Central Government in 1835. They demanded the restoration of the liberal Constitution of 1824 and the elimination of the dictator, Don Antonio López de Santa Anna.

Santa Anna was enraged. He personally took the field against the obstreperous *tejanos* ("Texans") in an attempt to squash the enemies of the fatherland. He drilled his men, and in the winter began the long march to San Antonio to put down the Texas Rebellion. He arrived at San Antonio in March, 1836, and on the 6th laid seige to the old Franciscan mission of the Alamo.

Mexicans and Texans died at the battle of the Alamo. Santa Anna destroyed every one of the defenders, both Mexican and gringo, and then proceeded to annihilate the garrison at Goliad. But Houston and the Texans had their revenge. At San Jacinto, Houston's army defeated Santa Anna's half-starved forces in less than an hour and eventually captured Don Antonio himself. Santa Anna, at pistol point, ordered the removal of Mexican troops from Texas soil and agreed to the formation of the Lone Star Republic. When Santa Anna returned to Mexico one year later, he welched on the deal and declared that Texas was, in fact, still a part of the Mexican States.

From 1837 until 1845 conditions in Mexico continued their chaotic course. Texas became a central issue in relations between Mexico and the United States, and Mexico threatened war should Texas be annexed to the Union. The Texans, at the same time, played footsie with England in an attempt to force annexation by the United States. The United States, however, faced its own internal problems, for the annexation of Texas would upset the balance between slave and free states. Both countries were primed for war by 1844. Santa Anna raised troops, and the United States approached the critical annexation with some trepidation. Finally, the annexation of Texas was consummated on March 1, 1845 and troops were readied in Mexico for the inevitable conflict with the Colossus of the North.

Meanwhile, in California, independence from Spain proved less jarring than it did for Texas. California was far away from Mexico, and the waves of political ferment that rocked Texas because of its close proximity to the arena of activity did not affect California in the same way. Yet, independence from Spain, in the eyes of many of the original *californios*, marked a sure decline in California's fortunes.

California in 1821 was one generation removed from the rough and ready pioneer stage, and its capital, Monterey, contained only 300 "rational people," or *gente de razón*. As a result, despite the protestations of those still wedded to monarchy and the Papacy, insidious liberalism from Mexico continued to creep into pristine California. The obvious generation gap occurred, and sons fought with parents about the validity of some of their fuddy-duddy ideas.

The introduction of liberal thought from Mexico and from the rest of the Western World for that matter brought about some interesting adaptations. First of all, religion became much less important and more formalized. One went to Mass only because it was expected rather than out of a sense of devotion to the Almighty. Of course, the women continued to attend devoutly but what else was there for a woman to do? Liberalism, writes Leonard Pitt, "was a satisfactory surrogate for religion and religious change probably prepared the Californians for a future life in a pluralistic society."

Fifteen years of liberalism in religion and politics extirpated royalism and fanatical Popery from California. Little resistance was encountered when the Franciscan missions were secularized, and most Californians viewed their position as extremely favorable vis-à-vis Mexico. In fact, the Californians denigrated the metropolitan Mexican and thought themselves a good notch or two above those unfortunates south of the Río Grande. California, along with other states of the Mexican federation, was strongly Federalist, and Mexican governors were often sent packing if they proved obdurate and inimical to California interests.

California, like other legatees of Spanish colonization, was an aristocratic hierarchic society. Its principal activity was ranching, and the ranchero maintained the same relationships with his *peones* that existed further south. Because of such parochial interests, family ties were omnipresent. One belonged to a family unit that occupied a certain geographic space in the California landscape, and this personal relationship often determined political alliances and attitudes. Contentment with things as they were characterized the *californio's* attitudes, and it was this hedonistic milieu that often offended and at the same time titillated Yankee traders in California.

As the flow of Yankees into California increased, everything they encountered at first horrified them. My God! those filthy greasers were aristocratic, they rejected work for its own sake, they were (Ugh!!) Catholic, and anyway, the poor fools were definitely inferior types in need of good, old American know-how. Generally, American witnesses who observed the California scene before 1846 manifested the Hispanophobia so typical of the Yankee milieu, and much of their writing and testimony was predicated on the idea that those poor bean bandits seriously needed annexation in order to uplift them through American tutelage.

The *californios,* however, proved more tolerant than their Yankee observers. They readily extended California hospitality to anyone that asked for it, even if he were an ignorant Yankee. Some Americans married into leading California families and were readily accepted as a part of the extended familial unit. Some *californios,* were they alive today, would classify as *Tíos Tacos,* the Chicano equivalent of an Uncle Tom.

By the mid-1830's, it became apparent that conflict between Mexican and American would occur. The polarized attitudes of individuals on both sides proved cohesive when war broke out with Mexico in 1846. In that year California would ultimately move to annexation by the United States, and the cultural conflict between *californio* and Hispano would be carried out on Yankee terms.

War between Mexico and the United States definitely erupted when troops of both countries clashed in the disputed territory between the Nueces River and the Río Grande. The initiation of the conflict between Mexican and gringo found both parties equally culpable, for both knew that the area was in dispute and both stationed troops there. Moreover, both countries were primed for war, and saber rattling was commonplace in Washington, D.C., and Mexico City. Therefore, abject apologias such as that enunciated by the late Senator Robert Kennedy a few years back seem strangely out of place. Kennedy apologized for the Mexican War and sang mea culpas for this poor, benighted country. Of course, this sort of hogwash is typical of the generation of politicians and scholars that want to bear the burden for historical phenomena that today are viewed with some disdain. But, I digress.

The Mexican War proved a disaster for Mexico. Her internal politics placed Santa Anna back in power, her treasury was devastated, and his armies suffered innumerable indignities at the hands of Zachary Taylor and Winfield Scott. The Treaty of Guadalupe Hidalgo that ended the war in 1848 gave approximately half of Mexico's territory to the United States. In 1853, the Gadsden Purchase ceded to the United States the Mesilla Valley; this was Santa Anna's final act of truncation against the country that he served so generously and so badly.

The entire conflict between Anglo and Hispano between 1700 and the consummation of the Mexican War in 1848 underscored the essential conflict between the two cultures. Both countries underwent serious throes of nationalism in the first decades of their existence, and these conflicting nationalist views clashed ultimately. On the Mexican side, they viewed the Yankee as aggressive and lacking soul, too intent upon making a bundle of money and devoid of humanity.

The gringo view of the Mexican was a legacy of the long conflict between England and Spain. Those filthy little greasers were Catholic, they eschewed labor and industriousness, and generally needed to be uplifted. This, of course, became a general American attitude and demonstrated an irreconcilable chauvinism. By God, those Mexicans would be improved through Yankee ingenuity, whether they wanted it or not. As a result, with the borderlands firmly in the United States hands, the conflict between Anglo and Hispano would continue, with the Anglo becoming the dominant cultural element. It was, argued the Anglos, their manifest destiny to uplift the little brown brethren even if it meant stealing their land and tinkering with their cultural ways.

Say, what's "la causa"?

3

Adaptation and Conflict, Mexican-Americans and Anglos, 1848-1910

Mexicans living in Texas, California, New Mexico, Arizona, and parts of Utah and Colorado awakened one day to discover that they no longer resided in Mexican territory. Rather, a successfully prosecuted war by the United States had converted them into at least residents of that victorious country. In Texas, annexation took place in March, 1845; California would achieve statehood in 1850 while Arizona and New

31

Mexico moped around until 1912 to enter the Union as full-fledged entities. While the Treaty of Guadalupe Hidalgo ostensibly guaranteed the rights—political, economic, and cultural—of resident Mexican groups in the newly acquired territories, the more practical problems of adaptation to a new and different body politic made the provisions of the treaty temporarily meaningless.

For Mexicans or *californios* in California, Mother Nature foisted a cruel twist to their attempts to adapt to United States control. The discovery of gold at Sutter's Fort in 1848 and the subsequent gold rush of 1848-1849 saw a massive movement of Anglos into the new territory. The '49ers moved into the California gold fields, devouring everything upon which they could lay their grubby hands. At the same time, *californios* attempted to cash in on the golden largesse that California's streams spewed forth and also attempted to lay substantial claims to gold rich streams.

Conflict inevitably ensued. Claim jumping, the harassment and physical mistreatment of Mexicans and *californios* in the gold fields, and the conscious exacerbation of resentment created a polarity between the conquering Anglos and the less than supine *californios*. Complicating the relationship between Anglo and *californio* in the tense gold-drenched situation was the presence of Mexicans, primarily from Sonora, who successfully extracted gold from the hills and streams of northern California.

These Sonorans, many of whom were experienced miners, joined the exodus to California and the opportunities for a get-rich-quick life. Sonorans, in the eyes of the *californios*, were no better than peons. The *californio* disdain for things Mexican could be traced to the 1820s and 1830s and persisted into the American period. Yet, the Anglos could not or would not distinguish between *californios*, Sonorans, or any Spanish speaking type, including Chileans, when "greasers" were excluded from the gold fields. Acts of violence and acts of reprisals characterized the period. By 1849, over 100,000 new people arrived

in California hoping to enrich themselves and live happily in
an Elysian paradise lined with California gold.

The influx of immigrants into California necessitated the
creation of a more extensive civil government than could be
provided by the territorial government in power. The calling
of a Constitutional Convention in 1848 saw eight of the forty-
eight delegates composed of *californios*, including the noted
Mariano Vallejo, a pronounced Yankeephile and major land
holder in northern California.

It has been assumed that somehow the eight *californios*
conned the other forty delegates to provide the former Mexican
citizens with their civil rights. No doubt the presence of Vallejo
and his cohorts reminded the other delegates of a bicultural situation now extant in California. The Constitution provided
for the printing of all laws in Spanish as well as English. Yet,
it is unreasonable to argue that had the Anglo delegates not
been inclined to grant a recognition of cultural validity to the
californios that eight Mexicans, no matter how persuasive,
could have dissuaded them from an utter emasculation of
californio rights.

While a Pyrrhic constitutional victory might have been
won in 1849, *californios* faced a more practical battle. Squat-
ters, disgusted with their inability to find gold, seized lands
from the sprawling and ill-defined ranchos and claimed them
for their own. Land disputes arose, and the United States
Congress jumped into the act with the passage of the Land Act
of 1851. This act, intended to clarify titles, in actuality worked
against the *californios*. Venal judges, collusion between attor-
neys, and an increasing anti-Mexican sentiment in California
led to significant reductions in the sizes of most of the original
ranchos. Added to the reduction in the amount of acreage, the
rancheros were faced with staggering legal fees that forced
them to collateralize their lands in order to pay off their law-
yers. Many a barrister in California enriched himself during
the 1850s defending *californio* claims under the Land Act of
1851.

Increased squatter activity intensified anti-Mexican feeling in California. Some *californios*, unable to rationalize the control of their areas by foreigners, took to the hills in order to gain some advantage through banditry. The legendary Joaquín Murieta, of whom there were plentiful claimants to the role, emerged as a Robin Hood stealing from the rich Anglo to give to the oppressed Mexican. This is nice mythology but not very accurate reality, for Joaquín was a thief who, had he been operating in pre-Anglo days, would have been as much a persona non grata as he was in the 1850s. The cultural tension created by the Anglo presence permitted Joaquín and upstanding citizens like Three Fingered Jack García to pillage the countryside with altruistic proclamations but with penurious intent.

Of course, dudes like Three Fingered Jack and Joaquín gave all Mexicans one very bad press. Even in the 1840s and 1850s the Anglo was not quite bright about cultural subtleties. Obviously, all Mexicans were like these two notorious bandits. Therefore, all Mexicans should be dealt with accordingly. As a result Mexicans were ripped off, had their lands stolen, their women violated, and their culture mocked. Yet, the creation of this polarity resulted from mutual animosity held by some Anglos and some *californios*. Reactions on both sides were violent. Representatives of both sides disliked their opposite number and created a series of myths about the rapacity, viciousness, and unique cruelty of their antagonists.

Most of the anti-Mexican, anti-Anglo activity occurred in northern California prior to the Civil War. In southern California, an area that was not particularly hospitable, the adjustment between Anglo and *californio* came more gradually and proved less jolting. For one thing, lack of gold and a shortage of water kept Anglos out of southern California. In addition, immigrants from Sonora came to southern California and helped maintain a Spanish-speaking majority in the area. Finally, economic prosperity shared by Anglo and *californio* made the adjustment a little more palatable. Cattle drives from Texas and Sonora gave immense prosperity to the area. This, however, was cut short by droughts. All was not wasted, however, for southern California diversified its agriculture, initiated irrigation systems, and emerged as a multi-purpose agricultural area.

Meanwhile, Anglos and Mexicans in Texas also found themselves in conflict. Relations between Anglos and Mexicans in Texas increased in acrimony initially because Texas had been the original battleground between Mexicans and Anglos. In part, the tension resulted from the southern origins of most of the Texas settlers. Their racial attitudes tended to thrust the Mexican into an inferior status. Among Mexicans themselves there occurred tension with regard to racial and social origins. Descendants of original Spanish inhabitants of Texas, referred to as *tejanos,* looked disdainfully at newly arrived Mexican immigrants. Both *tejanos* and Anglos treated the Mexican as inferior.

Like the *californios,* many upper class *tejanos* intermarried with the Anglos during the period of Texas independence and immediately after annexation in 1845. Some cultural hybridization thus occurred. Neither *tejano* nor Anglo thought much of the lower class Mexican. Both groups in the upper strata of society believed in the essential stratification of society and viewed the lower classes as in their proper places.

The Río Grande, now a part of the international boundary between Mexico and the United States, did not provide a barrier to unlimited immigration to Texas. Increasing numbers of Mexicans entered Texas as political instability in Mexico made life in that country increasingly untenable. The increase of Mexicans in Texas, especially south Texas, heightened tensions, saw an upswing in general lawlessness, and made life hell for the majority of peaceful Mexicans, who, like those in California, were stereotyped as malignant Frito Bandidos.

One excellent example of the animosity felt vis-à-vis Mexicans was the Cart War of 1857. The trade from San Antonio to the Texas coast had always been brisk since Spanish times. With a growing population in central Texas, more goods were needed from Texas ports. Mexican freighters excited the antagonism of newly arrived Anglo competitors because of Mexican superiority in this field of endeavor. Consequently, Mexican pack trains were devastated, goods stolen, freighters shot up. Anglo vigilante action coupled with an increased presence of federal troops quickly stopped the depredations.

Texas also possessed its version of Joaquín Murieta, except this one was identifiable and probably motivated by some degree of altruism. Juan Nepomuceno Cortina, "Cheno," scion of a wealthy family in Tamaulipas, excited public attention when he raided Brownsville, Texas, on September 28, 1859, seeking vengeance for the wrongs done to his fellow Mexicans living in Texas. Cortina and his men took over the town and shot it up, killed three Americans, attempted to raise the flag of Mexico on United States soil in symbolic protest, and then left. Cortina and his crew issued proclamations against the Anglos. Increased presence of United States troops in Brownsville eventually kept Cortina from crossing the border again.

Such a setback, however, failed to deter Cortina. Now a hero in the eyes of Mexicans living on both sides of the border, Cheno continued his forays into Texas. In the 1860s he succumbed to temptation, became governor of Tamaulipas but continued to support covertly excursions into Texas. Hotheads like Cortina, however, retarded attempts by both Anglos and Mexicans to achieve some sort of working relationship in Texas.

In New Mexico, however, the converse situation existed. Rich Hispanos, or *ricos*, made quick alliance with the Anglo conquerors of New Mexico. To the *ricos* it was a matter of survival. If their compliant acceptance of Anglo rule allowed them to retain their lands and riches, it was a small price to pay for the retention of traditional perquisites. To be sure the new Anglo inhabitants of New Mexico found the stratified society abhorrent. To them, an articulated class system seemed more repugnant than the de facto social aristocracy that existed in the eastern United States.

Another factor that affected the Hispano acceptance of Anglo rule was the virtual rejection of Mexico by the Hispano inhabitants of New Mexico. The *ricos* and even some of the lower classes viewed themselves more as Spaniards than Mexicans and felt little if any loyalty to a government in Mexico City that was beset with chaos and incapable of maintaining even a semblance of order in its distant territories. While the anti-Mexican attitude was not universal, especially along the newly created United States-Mexican border, the principal New Mexican leaders around Santa Fe opportunistically cooperated with the American arrivals to New Mexico.

Still, some dissension manifested itself in violence. In Taos, a Mexican and an Indian plot was suppressed in 1846. In the following year a rekindled rebellion resulted in the murder and scalping of the American governor. Ringleaders of the revolt were captured, tried, and hanged for treason after their violence led to the destruction of other Anglos or pro-American Hispanos.

The swift suppression of the Taos rebellion and the subsequent execution of its leaders engendered ill will among some Hispanos. Such animonsity was, however, short-lived, for the American government intervened eventually when Texas attempted to annex the eastern part of New Mexico. Maneuvers by Texans, beginning with a Texas annexation law in 1848 and a commission to organize eastern New Mexico politically in 1848, proved abortive. In 1850, New Mexicans convened a constitutional convention in an attempt to garner statehood. The United States Congress, however, refused to grant statehood to New Mexico because of the precarious balance between free and slave states and instead made New

Mexico a territory. Such action granted to the area a territorial legislature in which leading Hispanos, including Manual Otero and Father José Antonio Martínez, played prominent roles throughout the 1850s.

Massive territory once belonging to Mexico entered the Union at a time when the United States moved closer to fratricide. Conflicts between slave and free states polarized political opinions, and economic strife within the established states of the Union eventually erupted in civil war in 1861. In the newly acquired territories of California, the Southwest, and Texas, the Mexican-Americans reflected also some of the strife extant in other parts of the country. Generally, most of them remained loyal to the Union. In California, some Mexican-Americans volunteered for service with Union forces. In New Mexico the fear of Confederate Texas brought about some feelings of loyalty toward the Union. Those few Mexican-Americans who did support the Confederacy, especially in New Mexico, found themselves dispossessed of their goods and properties after the defeat of the South.

Meanwhile, Mexico, despite her disastrous defeat in the war with the United States, found it a congenital impossibility to achieve a modicum of stability. Mexico's humiliation in 1848 demoralized the government and the country in general. A succession of colorless and incompetent presidents ascended the presidential chair at Chapultepec until 1853 when Antonio López de Santa Anna, much of the cause of Mexico's grief, returned from exile to assume dictatorial powers once again. In this Santa Anna readily recognized the need for money.

In the original settlement of Guadalupe Hidalgo the Mesilla Valley still remained Mexican turf. Santa Anna sold the Mesilla Valley or the Gadsden Purchase to the United States in 1853 in order to finance his payments to a venal court and to an army that cried for wages and perquisites.

The sale of the Gadsden Purchase rekindled nationalistic impulses in Mexico. Opposition to Santa Anna began to spread and in 1854, coalesced around a rugged old Indian soldier, Juan Alvarez. Alvarez was joined by other malcontents in the issuance of the *Plan de Ayutla* that served as a banner for opponents to Santa Anna. By 1855, Santa Anna again fled into exile, Alvarez served as provisional president, and a plethora of new liberal leaders appeared on the scene.

Principal among these new leaders was Benito Juárez, a Zapotec Indian from Oaxaca. Juárez and his associates proved instrumental in the writing of an anti-clerical set of laws that reduced the power of the Church and made it subservient to the State. This end, a long-held wish of Mexican liberals, was accomplished between 1855 and 1857. Special privileges, or *fueros*, were taken from the clergy and military. Church lands not used directly for worship were disamortized, and the civil activity of the clergy underwent regulation. Added to this was a new Constitution written in 1857. In 1858, Juárez succeeded to the presidency of Mexico.

Opposition to Juárez emerged almost immediately. Clergy and conservative laymen found Juárez anathema to the continuation of traditional values in Mexico and launched a revolt against him. The so-called *Guerra de la Reforma,* or War of the Reform, pitted Juárez, now on the run, against Conservatives who had taken over Mexico City. In this the United States remained constant and continued to recognize the peripatetic Juárez government.

The War of the Reform lasted for three years. Yet, peace would not come to Mexico. Conservative connivers, desirous of a monarchy in Mexico and shocked by the recovery of Juárez, persuaded Louis Napoleon of France to sponsor a prince for a nonexistant Mexican throne. The groundwork was well laid for a French takeover of Mexico. Upon the pretext of collecting long standing debts, France, joined by England and Spain, invaded Mexico in 1862. England and Spain, however, quickly saw the French motive and withdrew from the expedition.

Between 1862 and 1867 France, aided by Mexican conservatives, controlled significant parts of Mexico. Juárez and his embattled liberals were driven north into Chihuahua to carry on guerrilla campaigns against the Mexican emperor and the French. In this endeavor, Juárez received assistance from Mexican-Americans, many of whom joined his guerrilla forces or who supplied him with arms and money to continue the struggle. At the same time, Juárez retained the official recognition of the United States.

The French Intervention in Mexico fanned flames of Mexican nationalism. Benito Juárez became the symbol of the embattled liberal fighting against the forces of oppression and obscurantist monarchy. Slowly but surely Juárez and his forces fought their way south to Mexico City and eventually drove out Maximilian's supporters. The emperor himself was captured and executed at Querétaro in 1867.

There is no doubt that Juárez was the principal element in the removal of the French from Mexico. It should also be noted, however, that the United States and Prussia both contributed to the evacuation of Mexico by French forces. In the case of the United States, civil war raged until 1865. While Secretary of State William H. Seward lodged protests about the French presence in Mexico, he could not go too far for fear of alienating Louis Napoleon. Such a move might provoke French recognition of the Confederacy. In Prussia, Otto von Bismarck began maneuvers that threatened France on her eastern borders. As a consequence, with troops committed all around the globe, she needed those forces stationed in Mexico to protect herself at home.

It was, however, Juárez who served as the prime mover in a renewed Mexican nationalism. Foreign pressure and intervention acted as the spark that lighted nationalistic fires. For this Juárez deserves the deepest reverence from his countrymen. But this act alone does not merit his secular canonization by Mexican officialdom nor by Mexican-American militants who see in Juárez the personification of *mexicanidad*.

Juárez as a man and Juárez as a national myth seem

inseparable. His adulation by Chicano elements in the United States stems from his successful ouster of the French and from the fact that Juárez was an Indian. It is in this latter category that the shibboleths of the Chicano militants become apparent. By declaring Juárez the quintessence of Mexicanness, there emerges a total rejection of Mexico's Iberian past. This Indianist tendency both in Mexico and among Chicanos means that one half of Mexico's heritage is forgotten. Juárez becomes the destroyer of monarchic evil, the defender of democracy in Mexico, the slayer of ecclesiastical dragons.

Without a doubt Juárez achieved some of these ends. Ultimately, however, he was but another authoritarian Mexican politician. Despite pronouncements about electoral will, Juárez struggled for reelection in 1872 only to die after his very close victory over Porfirio Díaz and Sebastián Lerdo de Tejada. Of necessity Juárez acted as he did. He was a shrewd politician, pragmatic, cunning, ruthless. Rigidity of mind also characterized Benito the Man. His utter refusal to have any truck with the military indicated a refusal to compromise. With a disaffected and partially unemployed military on his hands, Juárez, for the remainder of his days, lived under the Damocletian sword of armed revolt, a worry that he partially could have prevented. Yet, Juárez' supporters, both in Mexico and in the United States, view this intransigence as adherence to high principle. From one point of view, Juárez ultimately created a situation that allowed Porfirio Díaz to dominate the country for thiry-five years. The chaos that followed Juárez after the defeat of the French posited but one alternative for Mexico: order at the sacrifice of personal liberties. Juárez merits a great deal of respect from his countrymen and from Chicanos; his memory does not, however, deserve the insult of a dehumanizing, invalid form of secular canonization.

Throughout California, the Southwest, and Texas, the

aftermath of the Civil War in the United States and subsequent readjustments ushered in a new phase in the development of the Mexican-American. In California, massive railroad construction in the 1870s and 1880s provided jobs for Mexican-Americans as well as imported Chinese coolies. At the same time, the railroad boom further whittled away the old land grants held by the original *californios*. In other ways too the *californio* culture became diluted. By 1900 only pockets of *californio* culture remained viable. The sudden immigration from Mexico after 1910 would reenforce Mexican culture in California.

To many Mexicans, going to California was a volitional act, something for which one made careful plans. With regard to Texas and the Southwest, a marked difference in attitude prevailed. Nearly 2,000 miles of common border between Mexico and the United States, often noted merely by lonely markers in the desert, proved inviting to Mexicans wishing to get into the United States to escape circumstances at home. Conversely, Mexico proved a refuge for those Anglos who ran afoul of the law in Texas, New Mexico, and Arizona. A virtual open border created a subculture in the Southwest with minimal bilingualism and with some common attitudes about individuality and economic life.

In Texas a cattle boom slowly made its impact after the Civil War. By the late 1870s Texas became the principal supplier of beef for the Eastern United States. Texas influence in the Great Plains and Rocky Mountains could be seen in the manner in which cattle were handled by the American cowboy. Yet in Texas much of the cattle handling was still done by the original husbandmen: the Mexican vaqueros.

The Texas cattle industry, in fact the entire range cattle industry in the United States, became a direct legatee of husbandry practices utilized in Mexico before the arrival of Anglos into Mexican territory. Language, the principal vehicle of culture, was perpetuated in the Southwest. Lasso, lariat, corral,

remuda—all are of Mexican-Spanish origin and persist today
in the parlance of contemporary cattlemen.

Of greater import, however, than quaint language and
practices was the relationship between the cattle industry in
former Mexican territories and that same industry in northern
Mexico. The beef boom of the 1870s and 1880s in the United
States found that country with a beef deficiency. As a result,
Mexico's beef cattle industry grew in order to supply a demand in the United States. Mexicans on both sides of the border actively participated in the handling of cattle destined for
Eastern markets. Eventually a reasonably workable symbiosis
developed, only to be disrupted by the Mexican Revolution of
1910.

With regard to Texas and New Mexico, the introduction
of sheep production on a commercial basis for both meat and
wool produced active participation by Mexican-Americans. In
Texas an expansion of railroads provided markets for Texas
wool and pressure increased for greater output. The Mexican
sheepherder proved the ideal handler of Texas sheep. The wool
boom provided increased employment for Mexicans residing
in Texas.

A greater stimulant to immigration from Mexico to Texas
before 1910 appeared in cotton culture. North from Mexico
came immigrants to work on the cotton plantations of east and
central Texas. Mexicans and Mexican-Americans competed
with Blacks and poor whites in the cotton fields, and racial-
ethnic tensions grew in the area.

New Mexico also received its share of bad men and senseless violence. Like Texas and California, Anglo violence was
matched and often exceeded by Hispano retribution. The
Lincoln County War of 1878 saw sheepmen and cattlemen
using Mexicans for target practice. Only a general amnesty
declared by the military governor, General Lew Wallace,
brought about some peace and order. It was here that the in-
famous William Bonney, or Billy the Kid, added so many

notches to his gun, not a few of which were counted on Mexicans. Finally, in 1881, Sheriff Pat Garrett ambushed the pimply-faced killer and gave a coup de grace to widespread Anglo violence.

Hispanos in New Mexico also produced their supposed heroes. Elfego Baca, a man who would later become Sheriff of Socorro County, won fame and notoriety by holding off a mob of eighty Texans, killing four and wounding a score. Another of this ilk was obviously deranged: Sostenes L'Archeveque, a son of Mexican and French parents, went around the bend when his sweet old daddy was killed by Anglos. L'Archeveque wiped out twenty Anglos in retaliation for the death of his father. However, his prowess with firearms proved his downfall. Hispanos ambushed him and dispatched him to his forebears; they feared that L'Archeveque's unbridled violence would bring Anglo recriminations on them.

These incidents, however, were generally isolated. New Mexico, like Texas, in the post-Civil War period experienced a fantastically profitable cattle boom. Transcontinental railroads penetrated the state in order to facilitate the marketing of New Mexican cattle. As Apaches and Comanches were pacified, economic empires composed of cattle, mining, and lumber sought more land in order to expand activities. As a result, Anglos and Hispanos, lacking the legal and political wherewithal to resist corporate encroachments, lost their lands.

A sheep industry began to boom in New Mexico as well. Hispanos along the upper Rio Grande valley moved to the New Mexican grasslands. Here, as in Texas, they contributed to an expanding demand for wool and lamb. The *partido,* or shares system of sheep ranching, seemed like sharecropping in the post-Civil War South.

All things, however good, must come to an end. The cattle and sheep booms fizzled. Anglo ranchers began to compete with Hispanos for the rich grasslands in an attempt to eke out a living. In 1891, the federal government aggravated the problem when it set aside millions of acres of New Mexico as national forests. Grazing on these lands was thus restricted and limited the amount of beef and wool production that these lands could yield.

Despite limitations on available land in the 1880s and 1890s, Anglos continued to enter New Mexico in droves. Many Hispanos retreated to cultural enclaves rather than accept assimilation. Cultural isolationism was merely the benign response of the Mexican-American to increasing contact with the Anglo in New Mexico.

Other reactions smacked of gang warfare. *Las Gorras Blancas,* or the White Hats, were a Hispano Ku Klux Klan, intent on giving a vengeful hell to Anglo evildoers. This outfit proved so troublesome and was blamed for so many atrocities that in the 1890s it was declared illegal by the territorial governor. To back up his declaration, the governor promised to use the militia and, if necessary, federal troops to disband *Las Gorras Blancas.*

The other group, *La Mano Negra,* or the Black Hand, smacked of something straight out of a Mafia movie. Like the *Gorras Blancas,* they terrorized homesteaders who, through fencing their sections of land, inhibited the passage of Hispano sheepmen. Like the Gorras Blancas, they destroyed railroad property and generally committed acts of violence and depredations aimed at hassling the Anglo.

Land emerged as the key to conflict in New Mexico. After the Civil War politicians in Santa Fe, aided by *rico* families, proceeded to commit a monumental rip-off. Millions of acres of New Mexico's land ultimately fell into the hands of the Santa Fe Ring. Historical flukes as well as federal intervention connived to aid the Santa Fe Ring in its acquisition of land grants. In 1891, Congress created the Court of Private Land Claims for New Mexico, Colorado, and Arizona. For New Mexico, proving title was difficult. The Pueblo Revolt of 1680, the removal of archival records in 1846 by retreating Mexican troops, and the destruction of the New Mexico Archives for lack of space in 1869 and 1870 made the verification of title nearly impossible. By 1894, approximately 80 percent of the land grants were owned by Anglos.

Another major bone of contention in New Mexico was religion. California and Texas did not experience the religious strife that faced New Mexico shortly after its acquisition by the United States. The first Bishop of New Mexico, a French Jansenist by the name of Jean Baptiste Lamy, proceeded to alienate the few Hispano clergy in the area and to encounter resistance to his attempts at Church reform. Bishop Lamy brought predominantly French clerics with him to New Mexico. Lamy and his perfumed priests generally conducted themselves condescendingly toward their Hispano parishioners and engendered a good deal of antagonism. One of those to be offended was Fr. José Antonio Martínez. Martínez, in a tiff, resigned his parish at Taos but continued to minister to the faithful. Lamy responded by suspending Martinez who ignored the order. He was then excommunicated. Again, to no avail. With Martínez' death in 1867, the schism ended. But the difficulties between Lamy and Hispano clerics indicated to the New Mexicans that the Church was a foreign element alien to their best interests.

New Mexico, like most of the northern provinces of Spain before 1825, suffered from a paucity of clergy. As a result, religion became a more mystical and individual experience. Such inward direction of religious experience became ripe ground for a fanatical organization known as the *penitentes*. This group, often functioning in lieu of priests who were driven out by the liberal Mexican governments, took over sacerdotal functions. Once Lamy and his priests arrived, the *penitentes* became more and more secretive. Lamy failed to eliminate the group despite the reduction of its religious functions. The *pentitentes* then turned to politics and played footsie with the Republicans. When the order was officially disbanded in 1889, the group continued to meet in secret in order to carry out its religious activities. In addition, it contin-

ued as a powerful pressure group in the politics of New
Mexico.

New Mexico, probably more than California and Texas,
exemplified the desire of wealthy Hispano families to retain
some of their traditional perquisites. A *patrón-peón* labor
system continued to function as long as the *patrones* delivered
the votes to the proper place. Hispanos were well placed in the
territorial government. While the long territorial status of New
Mexico (until 1912) allowed for a continuation of the *patrón*
system, the underlying cause for the system and its perpetuation, despite the Anglo takeover, can be found in the cultural
milieu that was New Mexico. The *patrón* system was, primarily, a labor system predicated upon an idea of self-sufficient
units, like haciendas, producing a cash crop as well as everything necessary for subsistence. The relationship between
patrones and workers involved more than a boss-worker rela-
tion. Mutual dependence, both spiritual and temporal, existed.
An Anglo veneer on New Mexico did not alter the force of traditional relationships.

After 1870, while violence and the trauma of adjustment
struck former Mexican territories now in the United States,
Mexico slowly began to restore order to her shattered body
politic. In 1876, Porfirio Díaz, the military hero of the war
against the French, deposed Sebastián Lerdo de Tejada and en-
trenched himself in power. For thirty-five years Porfirio Diaz
ruled like a strong man in Mexico. Díaz, by coming to terms
with the bands of bandits, pacified the country. Failing to
reach agreement with intransigent bandits or military men,
Don Porfirio used more direct methods, including assassination, to eliminate malcontents.

The Mexican people, after over fifty years of chaos, welcomed the Díaz juggernaut. Those who eventually tumbled to
the fact that Díaz would sacrifice personal liberty for order and
peace usually fled to the United States and added to a growing

Mexican population there. Despite the rather brutal tactics used by Díaz and his henchmen, peace and prosperity came to Mexico. Mexico achieved budget surpluses. Her currency was highly regarded on world money markets. Foreign investment, encouraged by Díaz and his economic advisors, sought Mexico as a place for reasonably secure investment.

On this score, Díaz often sweetened the pot by handing over large tracts of land to foreigners in an attempt to encourage foreign enterprises in Mexico. It was here that the larger cattle companies—Palomas Land and Cattle Company, Corralitos Land and Cattle Company—received their start and were able to use Mexico as a further means of producing beef for a meat-deficient United States.

Of course, after thirty-five years, Díaz began to age. The Positivism that his group of advisors espoused proved sterile and a rationale for maintaining the lower classes in their places. Also, the massive foreign investments produced labor problems for Mexico. Urban and industrial labor began to make demands on management with accompanying managerial retaliation. Peasants began to demand lands. Poor Díaz! His advanced years robbed him of some of the political fire that had characterized his early maneuverings. Unwittingly, his success at bringing peace and prosperity to Mexico laid the groundwork for the most violent revolution in Mexican history, a revolution that would unseat Díaz and unleash mass action and mass mania onto the Mexican scene.

Between 1848 and 1910, Mexican-Americans as well as Anglos underwent a long period of traumatic adjustment. Anglos, feeling bitchy and superior about their recent conquest of Mexico's territory, looked with disgust on all Spanish-speaking people in the new territories. The Mexican-Americans responded in kind. They denigrated newly arrived Mexicans. Also, the Mexican-American response was of two

types. Some, like Mariano Vallejo of California, genuinely believed that the political processes introduced into the new territories by the United States would afford the original residents adequate protection. Others, those of a more violent
inclination like Three Fingered Jack García or Sostenes L'Archeveque, responded to the Anglo by shooting hell out of him.

The continuation of chaos in Mexico from the return of
Santa Anna until the emergence of Porfirio Díaz provided
some cultural reenforcement for Mexicans residing in the
United States. Mexican immigrants continued to come to the
United States in order to escape unsettled conditions in their
native land.

In addition, acculturation proceeded in the former
Mexican territories. Anglos soon adopted Mexican methods for
mining, ranching, and sheep husbandry and used the termi-
nology from northern Mexico for these enterprises. In this the
Anglo as well as the Mexican-American profited. In California and Texas, both Anglo and Mexican culture tended to
blend into a hybridized culture. New Mexico, however, proved
the exception.

In some respects the attitudes of the Hispanos of New
Mexico reflected in gigantic form the views of *tejanos* and
californios. All three looked with disdain on the newly arrived
Mexican. To them this toiler in the fields, this mine laborer
was a new arrival. He came to a land already settled and did not
have to risk his precious peasant neck to tame the land or the
Indians that tenaciously resisted its seizure. In Texas and California, the *tejanos* and *californios* blended with the new
arrivals. In New Mexico, however, the Hispanos remained distant and exploited the Mexican ruthlessly.

The first half century of American domination of the new
territories proved one of adjusting patterns of coexistence.
Hispanos in New Mexico tended to adapt more readily while at
the same time maintaining some of their cultural integrity. In

California and Texas, adaptation meant a dilution of the Hispanic culture. In sum, however, despite the violence, despite the unprincipled seizures of land by rapacious Anglos and equally rapacious Mexican-Americans, a reasonably workable arrangement had been achieved. This, however, would be severely disrupted by the outbreak of chaos once again in Mexico after 1910.

¡ Viva la revolución !

4

Revolutions, Migrants, and Depression, 1910-1940

Two stereotyped pictures exist of the Mexican. Either he is asleep against a cactus, a singularly uncomfortable position, or else he is armed to the teeth, bandoleros criss-crossing his chest, pistols in his hand, and an evil grin marking a mustachioed face. The former image derives from the idea that the Mexican is a slob, preferring to sit on his dead butt to working a good, Anglo eight-hour day. The other image finds its roots in the

51

violence of a massive revolution that shook Mexico between 1910 and 1920 with attendant aftershocks into the 1930s.

The Mexican Revolution (Upper Case R, please) began initially because young politicos wanted some of the political action. They were, however, joined by agrarian reform types, labor elements that suffered suppression under Díaz, and anarcho-syndicalists intent upon the destruction of everything that smacked of authority. The Revolution, therefore, needs to be dissected into its various phases and should not be viewed as a monolithic movement aimed at the total reformation of Mexican society, politics, and culture.

Mexico's revolutionary upheaval divides into three phases: 1910-1913, the overthrow of Díaz and the presidency of Francisco Madero; 1913-1915, the fight against Victoriano Huerta, a schism among revolutionary leaders, and the ultimate triumph of Venustiano Carranza; finally, 1915-1920, Carranza in power, the reduction of Pancho Villa to a regional nuisance, the writing of the Constitution of 1917, and the overthrow and death of Carranza in 1920. From 1920 until 1934, the revolutionary impulse emerges as a practical, pragmatic attempt to implement the articles of the Constitution of 1917 and for the new leaders of Mexico to maintain themselves in power. With the onset of a world-wide depression in 1929, changes occur within the revolutionary framework and by 1934 a radicalization of programs begins. From 1934 until 1940, Lázaro Cárdenas guides Mexico along radical paths to the solution of some of her internal problems. The first decade of the Revolution, however, has the most impact upon the United States and the Mexican-American, for it is here that old relationships suffer disruption and prejudices are exacerbated.

Mexico's epic revolution epitomized chaos. It began as an essentially political revolt against Porfirio Díaz and terminated in the total disruption of Mexican society, economy, and politics. When Madero, a most unlikely candidate to tackle the tough old caudillo, issued his *Plan de San Luis Potosí* in

October, 1910, from San Antonio, Texas, involvement of Mexicans on both sides of the border became immediate. Madero organized his rebellion in the United States; he sought support from resident Mexicans and Mexican-Americans in Texas, and made his triumphal reentry into Mexico in May, 1911, through El Paso-Ciudad Juárez. During this entire period Madero depended upon logistical support from backers in the United States.

In Mexico, northern revolutionaries established supply networks in the border region. Pascual Orozco, Jr., and Francisco Villa used El Paso extensively as a means of procuring arms and ammunition when they joined Madero in his fight against Díaz. In so doing, they set up liaisons with Mexicans sympathetic to the cause in the United States, a factor that facilitated the procurement of military ordnance.

Southern Mexico, especially the state of Morelos, proved of a different type. Emiliano Zapata had declared against Díaz in 1909. Zapata's support of the *Plan de San Luis Potosí* was tenuous, depending entirely upon Madero's vague promise of restoration of lands to those in Morelos who suffered deprivation by the *hacendados*. As a result, the relationship between the northern revolution and the agrarian revolution of the south was conditioned by the degree to which the northerners acquiesced in Zapata's demands for a monolithic agrarian reform.

Porfirio Díaz left Mexico in May, 1911. He was old, a bit senile, and suffering from a very bad toothache when he boarded the German vessel *Ypiranga* at Veracruz. Reputedly he declared about the Revolution: "Madero has unleashed a tiger; let's see if he can ride it!" Madero's inability to stay astride the symbolic pussycat presaged a decade of violence, death, and devastation for Mexico. It also forced a dislocation of Mexican-Anglo relations along the border.

When Madero assumed the presidency of Mexico in November, 1911, he already faced division among his former supporters. Zapata, for a variety of reasons, countered Madero's refusal to restore communal lands in Morelos with the *Plan de Ayala*. This *Plan* disavowed Madero as chief of the Revolution and elevated Zapata to that questionable honor. In addition, Orozco was in a sulk. As the principal military figure in Madero's success, Orozco felt that more revolutionaries should have been named to Madero's cabinet, including himself as minister of war. Instead, Madero stuck to those more of his inclination, namely, old-line politicos, family retainers, hangovers from the Díaz period.

Madero's indecisiveness allowed his detractors to make merry and prepare his downfall. As early as March, 1912, the situation continued to deteriorate. Pascual Orozco, Jr. declared against Madero, issued his own *Plan Orozquista*, and proceeded to disrupt northern Mexico. The United States responded to the Orozco rebellion with an absolute prohibition on the sale of arms to Mexico in order to keep the rebels from procuring weaponry. In addition, the Orozco rebellion split the revolutionary unity of the north. Pancho Villa threw his support to Madero.

During the Orozco rebellion, despite the prohibition on the sale of arms, both Orozco and Villa used the border as a means of obtaining armaments. Their contacts in El Paso arranged deals for the sale of weapons to the two leaders. To pay for these weapons cattle that roamed the great pastures of northern Mexico fell easy prey to *orozquista* and *villista* forces. These cattle were sold across the border, specie procured, and weapons purchased and smuggled into Mexico.

The Orozco rebellion did not last out the year. Federal troops under General Victoriano Huerta crushed the rebellion but failed to capture Orozco. By squelching the insurgency Huerta catapulted himself to prominence and paved the way for the eventual overthrow of Madero.

Madero continued to flip-flop in the presidency. He

lacked the necessary ruthlessness to eliminate his enemies and place his supporters in positions of power. As a result, the bureaucracy and most of the military were composed of individuals who attained their positions under Díaz. Don Porfirio's nephew, Félix Díaz, rebelled in Veracruz but was ultimately pardoned by Madero.

Meanwhile, Victoriano Huerta prepared the way for the elimination of Madero. As 1913 moved into its second month, Huerta made common cause with Félix Díaz and Bernardo Reyes, another old *porfirista*, for toppling the president. In this they were aided by the American Ambassador to Mexico, Henry Lane Wilson, a singularly unattractive diplomat. Wilson despised Madero as a disrupter of the peace imposed by Don Porfirio. He constantly sent reports to Washington denigrating Madero.

From February 9-18, Huerta and his cohorts steadily progressed in their objective of ousting Madero. Madero resigned the presidency on February 18, Huerta became provisional president, and Mexico stood shocked by coup d'etat once again. Four days later, Madero and his vice-president were mysteriously murdered while undergoing transfer from one prison to another. The murder of Madero elevated a political nincompoop to secular sainthood. Madero became in death what he could never achieve in life: the first martyr of the Revolution.

The image of the martyred saint rekindled the revolutionary ferment in Mexico. In northern Coahuila Governor Venustiano Carranza issued his *Plan de Guadalupe* and called all true believers to fight against Huerta, the usurper. His Constitutionalist banner rallied the greats of the Revolution— Pancho Villa, Alvaro Obregón, Emiliano Zapata (again tentatively). The Constitutionalist Revolution contained the seeds of continued turmoil for Mexico, for while Carranza and his crowd were united in their desire to overthrow Huerta they bickered constantly among themselves. Villa and Carranza were in constant conflict, and Obregón faced his own troubles on the west coast.

Northern Mexico and the United States Southwest again became the major staging areas for the Revolution against the government in Mexico City. Villa, with ruthless abandon, sold cattle to United States buyers in order to procure arms and ordnance. Most Constitutionalist commanders in the north used the simple expedient of stealing cattle, selling it in the United States, and buying their equipment there. Villa, however, because of his control of Ciudad Juárez, became the principal menace of cattle herds in Chihuahua or wherever his forces operated.

Throughout 1913 and into 1914 the Constitutionalist forces, especially Villa's *División del Norte* ("Division of the North"), pushed steadily toward Mexico City. Huerta found himself in a squeeze. Zapata continued to harass him in the South; the United States invaded Veracruz in April, 1914; Obregón moved in from the West; and Villa, who controlled the railroads in northern Mexico, moved inexorably toward the capital. Pressures on Huerta built up to a high pitch. In July, he resigned and went into exile in Europe.

The fall of Huerta failed to resolve the political problems in Mexico. Villa and Carranza were at loggerheads. By September, 1914, the rupture between them was irreparable. Mexico was about to be consumed by her revolutionary saviors. For the next thirteen months Villa and Carranza would contend for dominance in Mexico. Despite attempts to bring about a rapprochement between the warring factions, it took the defeat of Villa at Celaya in the spring of 1915 by Obregón to decide the ultimate victory of Carranza.

Villa, despite his defeats, continued to wage relentless war on Carranza. His ubiquitous presence in northern Mexico continually threatened Carranza's control of the country. In the South, Zapata, the chronic malcontent, denounced Carranza for his failure to restore lands in Morelos and to adhere to the agrarian principles of the *Plan de Ayala*. It was Villa, however, who posed the real threat.

In a fit of calculated pique, Villa raided Columbus, New Mexico, on March 9, 1916. In this he probably received some Mexican-American support. The raid forced the United States to send General John J. Pershing into Mexico with a Punitive Expedition to disperse and destroy Villa and his forces. The diplomatic problems that ensued between Mexico and the United States almost ensnared those two countries in conflict. Yet, Villa eluded his pursuers though Pershing did succeed in the dispersal of the *División del Norte*.

At the same time Carranza called a Constitutional Convention together in Querétaro in December, 1916. That body deliberated and produced a new and radical constitution for Mexico in February, 1917, that surpassed anything that the moderate Carranza hoped to achieve. Radical provisions governing land ownership, the Church, labor, education, and foreign interests in Mexico became a part of Mexico's organic charter. It was a nationalistic document; it jeopardized the odd position of foreigners in Mexico that had been established under Díaz.

For three more years Carranza ruled Mexico, increasingly dictatorial, evermore a modern personification of Porfirio Díaz. Saddled with a radical Constitution, Carranza immediately began to implement its most nationalistic provision— Article 27. His special target was the oil interests—mainly American and British—in Mexico. He circumscribed these with restrictions that finally led to increased difficulties between Mexico and the United States.

On Mexico's political front, by 1919 Obregón and General Pablo González made presidential noises. Carranza feared the popular Obregón and selected as his successor the mild Ambassador to the United States, Ignacio Bonillas. With a cry of imposition, Obregón, Plutarco Elías Calles, and Adolfo de la

Huerta, in April, 1920, issued the *Plan de Agua Prieta* that denounced Carranza as a dictator who attempted to thwart the electoral process. By late May, Carranza, in an attempt to flee Mexico City to Veracruz, met his death in a mud hut in a village called Tlaxcalantongo on the road to Veracruz.

Throughout the Revolutionary decade the United States, first under William Howard Taft and then Woodrow Wilson, attempted to cope with the phenomenon of modern revolution. Woodrow Wilson, especially, viewed it as his duty to instruct the less fortunate Mexicans in the art of government and as a result constantly meddled in Mexican affairs. A covey of special agents were dispatched to Mexico in order to send reports back to Wilson about the course of events in that country. Most of them were political appointees, deserving Democrats. Some were reasonably astute observers who found it difficult to write what Wilson wanted to hear when the facts did not necessarily conform to the presidential idea of what was proper for Mexico. Some agents were from the Department of State. The majority of them, however, were political coreligionists of President Wilson.

One of these agents originated in California, a descendant of an old *californio* family. Reginaldo F. Del Valle* (Anglicized to Reginald. Not much could be done with Del Valle unless he called himself Reginald of the Valley.) was a deserving Democrat. When he accepted the bid to go to Mexico, he was a member of the Los Angeles Public Service Commission. He supported William Jennings Bryan, then Secretary of State under Wilson, in his presidential bids and came out strong for Woodrow in 1912. Despite his fluency in Spanish and his Hispanic background, Del Valle could not be called an expert in Mexican affairs. He also possessed "the Spanish patricians' disdain for lower-class Mexicans, especially those of Indian

---

*Information on Del Valle is derived from Larry D. Hill. *Emisarries to a Revolution: Woodrow Wilson's Executive Agents in Mexico* (Baton Rouge: Louisiana State University Press, 1973), pp. 40-59.

blood." Furthermore, Del Valle was born with a big mouth.

Though the purpose of his mission to Mexico in mid-1913 was secret, strange accounts of his trip appeared in newspapers throughout the United States. He was identified almost instantly as an agent of Woodrow Wilson. Ostensibly Del Valle's mission aimed at helping the United States make policy decisions about how to confront the Mexican Revolution and the reaction against Huerta. In northern Mexico he interviewed revolutionary leaders. Officials in the Embassy in Mexico City wondered what in hell was going on.

While some revolutionaries viewed Del Valle as sympathetic to their cause, Venustiano Carranza, jealous guardian of Mexican nationalism, refused to credit Del Valle's Hispanicity with any merit. To Carranza, Del Valle was a Spanish-speaking gringo who wanted to come in to Mexico and direct the course of her internal affairs. Bemused but not thwarted, Del Valle then headed for Mexico City by the circuitous route of New Orleans and Veracruz.

Throughout his sojourn in northern Mexico, Del Valle gave extremely bad press to the revolutionary chieftains. Villa horrified him. He wrote off Obregón as a mediocrity. In general, he viewed them as sincere incompetents incapable of making democracy workable in Mexico. In central and southern Mexico, his mission became a disaster area. Preceded by a lot of brouhaha, Del Valle was rendered ineffective by his own big mouth.

Del Valle certainly granted the sincerity of revolutionary purpose. He doubted, however, the methods employed. His own patrician point of view recoiled at mass demands for land reform, confiscation of foreign property, the destruction of large enterprises. Essentially, Del Valle was a thoroughly acculturated *californio* who shared the view that free government was workable only with a viable middle class.

To more militant Chicanos Del Valle would appear as a *vendido*, a sell-out, a *Tío Taco* with bowler hat and spats serving as a sycophant to the dominant Anglo. That is one point of view. Granted that as a diplomat Del Valle bungled his mission. But to ascribe to Del Valle some sort of sell-out mentality is a refusal to come to grips with the historical realities. As a prominent *californio*, Del Valle, much like Mariano Vallejo before him, recognized the reality of United States acquisition of California and decided that cooperation with the new government and with those new interests was the only means for personal survival. Del Valle, moreover, possessed that *californio* attitude about Mexicans—they were indigent slobs. Such an attitude, while not commendable, is understandable within the context of Del Valle's background. He was a patrician, a believer in an ordered, aristocratic society. To upper class *californio* and the upper class Mexican the *indio* remained at the bottom of the heap because of some genetic inferiority. Yet, Reginaldo del Valle merits some consideration. He symbolized the way in which some Mexican-Americans adapted to ways of life in territory that formerly belonged to Mexico. In some respects, Del Valle is the reverse of the Chicano coin. While not rejecting his mother culture, he comfortably operated in a bicultural setting.

Mexico's epic revolution of 1910-1920 brought about drastic changes along the border, in the country itself, and upon Mexican relations with the United States. Approximately one million Mexicans legally or illegally entered the United States during the decade. Many of these immigrants left their native land in order to escape the chaos engendered by the Revolution. Inflationary prices, fear of starvation, the dread of having one's land and goods forcibly taken, and the fear of violent death contributed to the reasons that Mexicans entered the United States. In addition, the factional strife that characterized the Revolution after 1913 sent supporters of losing factions into the United States, fearful that the victors might begin vendettas against them.

The loss of nearly one million inhabitants as a result of emigration cost Mexico dearly in the 1920s. As the process of stabilization began after the violent phase of the Revolution, the dominant faction in power was loathe to allow some of the exiled talent back into the country. There were, of course, notable exceptions, among these José Vasconcelos, who served as Minister of Education under Alvaro Obregón (1920-1924), and Martin Luis Guzmán, the noted Mexican novelist. These two men had both served the Convention government that was so dominated by *villistas* and *zapatistas* during the struggle for dominance against Carranza.

Along the border, especially in Texas, Mexican immigrants moved into Mexican-American enclaves. The tensions brought about by the Revolution led both Mexicans and Mexican-Americans to form pressure groups in the United States in support of one or another faction in Mexico. These groups, at least from a cursory survey of available evidence, used political pressures upon American politicians in order to influence United States policy vis-à-vis the Revolution.

In addition, the polyglot nature of the increased Spanish-speaking population of the Southwest between 1910 and 1920 necessitated the creation of increased organs of communication. Plethoras of Spanish language newspapers sprang up along the border. Some of these were founded and edited by Mexican-Americans. Others were the creation of Mexican journalists who had fled Mexico.

Principal among these Mexican emigré journalists was Silvestre Terrazas. Terrazas belonged to a cadet line of the family of Don Luis Terrazas, the immensely powerful *hacendado* of Chihuahua. When Huerta came to power in 1913, Silvestre Terrazas, whose politics were quite liberal and whose newspaper in Chihuahua City deplored the Huerta takeover, found it expedient to get out of town and head for El Paso. While there he founded a Spanish language newspaper and maintained contacts with other Spanish newspaper groups in the Southwest. This network of newspapers became an important factor in keeping the Spanish-speaking communities current with developments in Mexico. Terrazas and others like him remained in the United States after 1920 and contributed mightily to the reinforcement of Mexican culture in the Southwest.

Prior to the Mexican Revolution, relations between Mexicans and Anglos along the border achieved a tenable symbiosis that, while occasionally marred by mutual violence and prejudice, nevertheless held both groups together through mutual dependence. Economically, the border area served as a cohesive unit. A functional biculturalism existed. The Revolution disrupted this phenomenon. The sudden increase of Mexicans along the border in the Southwest brought prejudices into the open that affected the relations between the two groups.

Paradoxically, the increase in tension failed to destroy the economic dependence of both Mexicans and Anglos in this area. Mexican cattle continued to find a ready market in the United States. Mexicans continued to work in American enterprises along the border. Revolutionaries and counterrevolutionaries used the border as staging grounds for their enterprises. Most notable among these was Pancho Villa, whose network in El Paso kept him constantly supplied with arms, ammunition, and military ordnance. In addition, when Pascual Orozco, Jr., went into exile in 1912 he fled to El Paso. By 1914, after the downfall of Huerta, Orozco and the deposed dictator made common cause and planned a comeback using El Paso as a base of operations. Though the plan aborted in August, 1915, significantly the border served as an essential element in planning for a move against Carranza. Here could be found sufficient refugees of similar political persuasions; here could be found money and resources of supplies; here was a gateway to Mexico.

In part, the disruption of relations between Anglo and

Mexican along the border area resulted from the careless aim of Mexican rebels and soldiers. Stray bullets frequently crossed the border and killed or wounded curious American observers. Socialite hostesses in El Paso, for instance, used the rooftop of the Paso del Norte Hotel to have "revolutionary teas." Whenever a bullet came zinging by, it added to the increasing view of Mexican ineptitude.

Added to poor marksmanship was the problem of bandit and revolutionary depredations along the border. Bandits and rebels were in constant need of supplies. Small border towns and settlements combined with the large ranches that ran along the border and provided an illicit source of supplies for bandit and revolutionary alike.

After United States entry into World War I, the neutralist posture assumed by Mexico in that conflict provoked wide speculation in the United States that Mexicans were pro-German. Carranza certainly did nothing to dispel the notion that he favored Germany. As a consequence, a chauvinism in the United States grew that aimed directly at Mexico, at Mexican refugees, and at Mexican-Americans who had been longtime residents of the Southwest. In 1919, for example, the Senate Committee on Foreign Relations conducted inquiries into Mexican affairs. A principal avenue of investigation was the role of German agents in Mexico during the immediate prewar period and during the period of 1917-1918.

With the downfall of Carranza and ascension of Obregón in 1920, anti-Mexicanism along the border remained quite high. Because of complexities growing out of the Constitution of 1917, the United States refused to grant de facto recognition to Obregón until a series of unofficial contacts paved the way for a resumption of diplomatic relations in September, 1923. The issues at stake included the nonretroactivity of Article 27 and the payment of debts incurred by Mexico before and during the Revolution. Some elements along the border, however, viewed the Mexican predilection for loose women

and cheap booze as sufficient motive not to grant recognition
to the Obregón regime.

In the 1920s the United States indulged in its "Noble
Experiment" aimed at the elimination of Demon Rum from
the American diet. A moralistic fit prompted the passage of the
Prohibition Amendment and its enabling Volstead Act. For
citizens living along the border Prohibition proved a minor in-
convenience. Every weekend lines of cars waited patiently to
enter Mexico at Ciudad Juárez, Nogales, Tijuana, Nuevo
Laredo, and other border towns in order to obtain the for-
bidden elixirs of hops, grains, grapes, and the ever present
maguey plant, progenitor of tequila. Fundamentalist elements in the Southwest protested stridently to the Department
of State about the presence of fleshpots immediately south of
the border. In fact, some of these groups went so far as to advocate the withholding of recognition from Mexico until a dry
zone was established running at least one hundred miles south
of the international boundary. Luckily, State Department officials viewed this attitude as a bit loony and sent the usual sort
of noncommital reply. Yet, this attitude underscored the anti-
Mexican bias at work. Mexicans were by nature boozers, incapable of good honest work. Unless they cleaned up a bit, the
United States should not dignify their near-savage government with diplomatic recognition.

Despite a sort of extant nativism in the United States, the
newly arrived Mexicans provided a substantial pool of labor
for agricultural and industrial enterprises both inside and outside the Southwest. Within the southwestern area, the movement of Mexicans across the border into the United States did
not represent a change of nationality but rather the movement
into another part of a single cultural area. Increased opportunities in agriculture in Texas and California attracted many
Mexicans to work in the cotton and citrus fields of these areas
instead of living in the insecurity of a still unstable Mexico.
California by 1930, for example, possessed over one third of a

million Mexicans or Mexican-Americans, an increase of over 250 thousand in ten years.

From the Southwest, Mexicans and Mexican-Americans fanned out to industrial jobs. Chicago, for example, possessed the largest Mexican population outside of the Southwest. The burgeoning automobile factories of Detroit attracted Mexicans to higher paying jobs than could be found in agriculture. Steel mills in Pennsylvania employed significant numbers of Mexicans. The American railroad complex employed thousands of Mexicans.

Two immigration acts in 1921 and 1924 increased opportunities for Mexicans outside of the Southwest. These severely limited European and Asian immigration to the United States but imposed no quota on Mexican immigrants. As a result, American industry actively recruited Mexican and Mexican-American labor for various industrial enterprises.

Concomitant with the growth of Mexican employment in industry both inside and outside of the Southwest came the social problems attendant with every newly arrived immigrant group. Forced to compete with other ethnics in the different cities, Mexican barrios were soon established. Mexican grocery stores sprang up in Chicago and Detroit. City officials, however, were slow to respond to the needs of the new group. Church authorities did not particularly welcome the new arrivals. This attitude was especially prevalent among ecclesiastical officials of the Roman Catholic Church.

With rare exception, most of the Churchmen manifested a strongly anti-Mexican bias. These descendants of Irish immigrants were nurtured on Black Legend ideology and viewed anything Iberian as slightly less than human and given to all sorts of pagan obscenities. Consequently, Mexicans in the burgeoning barrios were forced to attend churches that did not want them, contend with clergy that failed to understand their culture, and raise their children in an environment that rejected Mexican culture and the Spanish language.

Additional impetus for the growth of a Mexican industrial force in the United States was the depressed state of agriculture in the Southwest. With the exception of California, Arizona, New Mexico, and Texas underwent an agricultural slump that failed to supply sufficient jobs for the thousands of migrant workers who depended upon this as a source of livelihood. As a result these workers, in combination with newly arrived Mexicans, went to industrial centers in search of employment.

California agriculture, however, provided a different story. California developed the Imperial and San Joaquín valleys during this period. Grapes, truck crops, berries, melons—a multitude of agricultural products—found rich soil in the great agricultural belts of California. Labor was needed. Consequently, the *enganchista* or *contratista*, a labor contractor, came into prominence. He was usually of Mexican descent. The *enganchista's* function revolved around the organization, recruitment, and placement of immigrant and Mexican-American agricultural workers. *Enganchistas* frequently ripped off their workers. Yet, they functioned within a cultural tradition that was comprehensible. The *enganchista* was very much like the labor *patrón* of the nineteenth century.

Between 1923 and 1925, the slump in United States agriculture abated. The initial postwar recession saw attempts to exclude Mexican immigrants in both 1921 and 1924; both of these failed. Nevertheless, a nativist tendency continued, and conflict between a powerful agricultural lobby and exclusionists ensued in Congress. In 1926 and 1927 bills were introduced in Congress, both in the House and in the Senate, that placed Mexican immigration on a quota system, a reversal of traditional United States policy that allowed open immigration to all Latin Americans. These attempts failed because of a powerfully organized agricultural demand for cheap labor.

By 1928, the flood of immigration increased from Mexico. Yet, lurking in the background was economic disaster. When the Great Crash struck in October, 1929, Mexican immigration virtually ground to a halt. No longer was the United States the happy hunting ground for Mexican immigrants in need of work. Even Mexican-Americans began to wonder if they had not been handed something of a rotten lemon. By the early 1930s, Mexicans resident in the United States began to seek repatriation and return to their native land. In this they were aided by Anglos who would have been happy to deport any Spanish surnamed individual.

When America's financial house of cards crashed in October, 1929, national trauma occurred. By 1933, 25 percent of the labor force was unemployed, and underemployment characterized millions of other jobs. The nation in general, and Mexican-Americans in particular, suffered from the result of excessive speculation and fiscal irresponsibility. The puncturing of the great industrial bubble of the 1920s left thousands of Mexican-Americans unemployed, and United States agriculture no longer provided the jobs of the previous decade. Crop and livestock production decreased, and Mexican-Americans were, consequently, without jobs. Regular and seasonal employment in the Southwest was drastically reduced, and bread lines grew.

In a contradictory way, urban Mexican-Americans returned to rural villages to attempt to eke out some sort of subsistence from the land. Conversely, some villagers fled to the city to take more rapid advantage of growing welfare programs. More rural villagers left for the cities than those returning to the villages. In New Mexico, for example, village population declined.

In addition, a variety of governmental programs inadvertently seized land from depressed villagers. In New Mexico, the Middle Rio Grande Conservancy District Project, established to make more land arable for agriculture, backfired. With the Depression, many Mexican-Americans could not pay the assessments and their lands were taken in forfeit.

Of even greater consequence for Mexican-Americans was the utter lack of employment and the discriminatory practices followed by some employers. Mexican-Americans found themselves in direct competition with Anglos for the wretched stoop labor of agriculture. Here were jobs that in the 1920s no Anglo would have touched. The Depression and the 1930s, however, changed all of that. Added to the competition were the Okie migrations from the Dust Bowl of Oklahoma. Anglo competed with Mexican for low paying jobs: but at least they were jobs.

In 1933, Franklin Delano Roosevelt became president of the United States. He ran on a platform of relief, recovery, and reform. Immediately, Roosevelt and his New Dealers sought to bring relief to millions of Americans. Like other Americans, the Mexican-American benefited most directly from this aspect of the New Deal. The Federal Emergency Relief Administration, the Works Progress Administration, the Civilian Conservation Corps—the whole plethora of alphabet agencies engendered by the New Deal—served the Mexican-American to some degree. Overall, however, Mexican-Americans benefited less from the New Deal than other Americans. In part, this resulted from an element of individual pride extant within the cultural group. The dole seemed a negation of the masculine role of providing a living for the family. Yet a significant number of Mexican-Americans did use federal, state, and local relief. As a result, another stereotype was added to the Mexican image: He was a bum who refused to work even with available jobs.

Meanwhile in Mexico, Lázaro Cárdenas became president in 1934. His massive reform programs called upon Mexicans to help in the restoration of the nation at a time of economic crisis. Added to a domestic call, Cárdenas called upon Mexicans living outside of the country to return to Mexico and aid in the rebuilding of the nation. Consequently, thousands of Mexicans stuck in the United States returned. In addition, some Mexican-Americans also returned. Even before Cárdenas came into power in Mexico, there were attempts to repatriate

Mexicans living in the United States. Transportation costs were paid to border points. Additionally, illegal immigrants were shipped back to Mexico. After Cárdenas came to power, another group of repatriates headed for Mexico. Mexican consuls in the United States actively sought out Mexicans who wished to return to Mexico. While the bulk of repatriates came from the Southwest and California, the Midwest also contributed a significant number.

Between 1930 and 1940, nearly half a million Mexicans and Mexican-Americans returned to Mexico. Most of these were not participants in the repatriation program established by Cárdenas. Consequently, very few of them received special consideration. By the late 1930s, however, some attempts were made to establish agricultural colonies for some repatriates. Repatriation, both forced and voluntary, did not achieve the objectives. It merely shifted an unemployed labor force from one country to another.

The entire period of the 1920s and 1930s began a growing agitation among Mexican-Americans in mining, agriculture, and industry. In the early 1920s, as agriculture suffered from postwar recession, tentative moves were made to organize agricultural workers. As late as 1927, the American Federation of Labor, meeting in Los Angeles, discussed the drawbacks to Mexican labor in the United States. The Federation of Mexican Societies responded by resolving that its member groups lend moral and financial support to any attempts to organize Mexican-American laborers. In response local groups organized the *Confederación de Uniones Obreras Mexicanas* (CUOM). This group was patterned after the CROM, the *Condeferación Regional de Obreros Mexicanos* in Mexico. Cultural reenforcement had again been given to Mexican-Americans by developments in Mexico. Despite some tentative support from the Mexican Government, the CUOM declined.

With the onslaught of the Depression and the devastation of agriculture in the 1930s, the discontent among migrant workers increased and provided fertile ground for radicalism. One radical grouping, the Cannery and Agricultural Workers Industrial Union (CAWIU), was affiliated with the Communists. Another radical outfit was the Trade Union Unity League (TUUL). Both of these contributed to unrest in southwestern agriculture. When combined with the indigenous discontent of Mexican-Americans, the labor situation in agriculture became volatile. TUUL actively recruited Mexican-American workers.

Countering outside radicals, indigenous radicals began to organize. In El Monte, California, the most successful agricultural union of Mexican-Americans, the *Confederación de Uniones de Campesinos y Obreros Mexicanos* (CUCOM) emerged as a result of a strike against berry producers in May, 1933. Local grievances in El Monte became targets for outside agitation from the radical CAWIU. The Mexican Consulate in Los Angeles proferred its assistance to local labor leaders who sought to counter outside radical influences. While the strike produced an agreement that guaranteed a minimum wage to berry pickers, the contract was consummated after the end of the berry season. Consequently, no immediate benefits accrued to the agricultural workers. In one respect, the workers did get something out of the strike: the organization of the CUCOM.

Throughout the 1930s, labor difficulties in agriculture had a direct effect upon Mexican-Americans. Attempts to organize agricultural workers were met with resistance by farm operators and chambers of commerce. Mexican workers were arrested and incarcerated in various instances. In part, the reaction of producers and businessmen resulted from the increased presence of the CAWIU. Intensified radical activity solidified resistance to agricultural unionization. By 1936 and 1937 the amount of radical activity among agricultural workers decreased, but opposition to agricultural unionization persisted.

Thirty years elapsed from the beginning of the Mexican Revolution until the eve of United States entry into World War II. During those three decades Anglos and Mexicans faced a disruption of established relationships. Prejudice on both sides acted to heighten tension. In addition, the massive increase of Mexicans in the United States in the 1910-1930 period forced United States nativists to attempt to keep Mexicans out and to discriminate against resident Mexican-Americans.

Additionally, the increased migration from Mexico and the restriction on European immigration in the 1920s provided a labor pool for industrial and agricultural expansion. After the onset of the Depression, Mexican and Mexican-American labor was forced to compete with out-of-work Anglos for some of the less rewarding jobs in agriculture.

One contemporary aspect of the impact of the Mexican Revolution on the Mexican-American movement is the adulation of certain revolutionary leaders as Chicano heroes. The two major figures are Emiliano Zapata and Pancho Villa. Zapata as a Chicano hero strikes an improbable chord. First of all, Zapata was from southern Mexico, the state of Morelos. His program aimed at the parochial interests of Morelos without relationship to the other impulses of the Revolution. When he attempted to impose his agrarian schemes on the rest of the nation by demanding adherence to the *Plan de Ayala*, lip service was paid to the impossible task of giving everyone his little chunk of land. It is difficult to deny Zapata his prominence within the context of the Mexican Revolution. While his schemes were inapplicable to the nation as a whole, they were probably workable in Morelos. Yet Zapata as Chicano culture hero is almost ludicrous. In the areas of Aztlán, the Hispano villages of New Mexico, the land reform programs of an Emiliano Zapata would prove most difficult to apply. While he was tenacious in adhering to his ideals, it also seems conceivable that Don Emiliano was a sufficient megalomaniac to believe that he possessed the total solution to Mexico's land problem. Reconciling Zapata with the Chicano hagiography remains difficult: he was a loser.

Villa was also a loser. But when he finally gave up the fight with the established government, it was on his terms. Villa also personified the temperament of northern Mexico. His rugged individualism and his tenacious defense of those elements of the northern ethos make him much more appealing as a hero for the Chicano movement. Of course, there exist elements of Villa's approach that are not socially acceptable. Homicidal rages and a mercurial personality make consistent policy a little difficult to pursue. Villa, as a result, suffered major defeats when he allowed the more primitive aspects of his character to dominate his thinking. Villa, moreover, personified the extreme nationalism of the violent period of the Mexican Revolution. His attack on Columbus, New Mexico indicated the contempt in which Villa held the United States. He also successfully evaded the Punitive Expedition, thus improving his stock among Chicanos. One aspect of Villa's anti-Yankee posture in 1916 is overlooked by his Chicano adulators. Prior to the recognition of Carranza, Villa, of all the revolutionary chieftains, proved the most cooperative with the misguided policies of Woodrow Wilson. Despite a personal admiration for Villa, in terms of singling out a hero for the Chicano movement Villa also fails to fit the bill: he too was a loser.

In terms of the Mexican Revolution and the Mexican-American, it would behoove Mexican-Americans to look toward their own for heroes more representative of their polyglot group. Mexico can provide basic reenforcement to Mexican-American culture, but it cannot supply substitutes for the truly autochthonous.

Braceros, Riots, and Awakening Consciousness, 1940-1960

Throughout the 1930s the Great Depression dragged on. Various agencies established by the Roosevelt administration attempted to bring a modicum of equilibrium to the depression-torn nation. Yet, by 1940 the nation still floundered in its internal economic problems. In Europe, however, the rapid and massive development of Germany under Adolf Hitler and the aggressiveness of the Nazis in Eastern Europe had, by 1939, plunged Europe again into war. By 1940, the United States moved closer and closer to involvement in the European imbroglio. Despite isolationist pressures to mitigate American involvement in Europe, Roosevelt and his administration strove to lend assistance to the beleaguered British. For the Western Hemisphere in general there existed a near consensus about the necessity of protecting the New World from insidious Fascist and Nazi influences.

For the Mexican-American the immediate prewar period saw him become increasingly involved in national economic recuperation. Though still neutral, the United States began to gear up for a wartime economy; more Americans joined the armed forces or were inducted; and industrial jobs went begging. The Mexican-American filled voids in industrial production. Companies and labor unions who were reluctant to accept Mexican-Americans in 1935 took them grudgingly in 1940 and 1941.

American neutrality, for all intents and purposes, became a myth by early 1941. De facto belligerency characterized the United States posture vis-à-vis the Axis powers. As 1941 rolled to a close it became merely a matter of time before the United States found itself involved in yet another world war.

Japan, the eastern link of the Axis connection, provided the reason for American entry into the war. On December 7, 1941, the Japanese destroyed Pearl Harbor, and the United States found itself at war with Germany, Italy, and Japan. The national preparations for aid to Britain provided the groundwork for the intensified national effort that would be required if America was to survive yet another global conflict within a generation.

American commitment to active participation in the war necessitated massive enlargement of the Armed Forces. Inductions and enlistments swelled the military ranks but left industries depleted of workers. In both agriculture and industry, the war demands of the military machine left jobs begging for workers to fill them. The Mexican-Americans generally enlisted in unprecedented numbers to fight against the maniacal Hun that overran Europe and the fanatical Imperial clique that devastated Asia. Consequently, industry and agriculture could not rely upon the normal labor pool of Mexican-Americans.

Some Mexican-Americans, however, found themselves lifted out of traditional environments and inducted or volunteered into Uncle Sam's Army. In New Mexico, for example, the Mexican-American had the highest per capita number of people in the Armed Services and also the highest number of enlistments. In addition, Mexican nationals residing in the United States joined the Armed Forces. Promised citizenship if they enlisted, many took the chance to serve their adopted country and at the same time acquire all of the perquisites of citizenship. President Manuel Avila Camacho of Mexico urged Mexican citizens in the United States to join the American military in order to stave off European dictatorship.

Many reasons exist for the high number of Mexican-Americans that were represented in the military during World War II. An easy route to naturalization was a basic motive. In addition, many draft-age youths in Mexican-American communities did not possess job deferments and consequently were inducted into the military. Futhermore, as in Mexico, the military provided a means of upward social mobility. While in some respects the Mexican-American still encountered prejudice and discrimination, the armed forces gave a broader perspective. On a very basic level, the Mexican-Americans were intensely patriotic. They volunteered more readily for the more hazardous branches of the Armed Forces, such as the paratroopers. Motivated in part by an unassailable machismo, Mexican-Americans during the war garnered the highest percentage of military honors, and their patriotism during a time of intense international strife was and is unquestioned.

With the increasing need for military personnel, domestic

industrial and agricultural production suffered from a lack of labor. Even with expanded opportunities, remaining Mexican-Americans could not fill the job void. Mexico, however, provided the manpower pool from which the United States would draw during the war period. As a part of Mexico's commitment to hemispheric cooperation during World War II, that country sent many of its needed workers to the United States in order to fill labor vacancies.

Of necessity the bracero program that involved the recruitment of Mexican nationals for labor in the United States composed two distinct phases: the exigencies of war time; and the postwar period that breaks down into individual subphases. The original law enabling passage of Mexican laborers to the United States was passed by Congress as Public Law 45, allowing up to 50,000 Mexican braceros to cross into the United States each year until December, 1947. Such an idea of regulated migratory labor from Mexico was not new at the time. In the 1920s such an idea had already been advanced, but Congress chose to ignore it. The 1930s, with its dust bowl migrations in the United States and with United States citizens competing for the dwindling supply of agricultural jobs, saw the idea shelved once again.

Approaching United States involvement in the war, however, emphasized the need for an increased labor pool. Reinstitution of military conscription in the United States removed laborers, both skilled and unskilled, from the industrial and agricultural areas and consequently began to create some labor shortages. The Japanese attack on Pearl Harbor placed greater pressure for laborers in American agriculture. Defense industry jobs robbed the agricultural producers of needed labor, and as a consequence they pressed for an open border policy of immigrant labor.

Mexico, however, did not prove instantly cooperative. The repatriation programs of the 1930s still rankled heavily in

Mexican memory, but the war time emergency forced a recon-
sideration by the Mexican government. A mixed committee of
Mexican and United States representatives began hammering
out an agreement as soon as Mexico declared war on the Axis
powers in May, 1942. By July, Mexico and the United States
signed an executive agreement that was ratified in Mexico City
within two weeks. In the provisions of the agreement constant
emphasis appeared about the temporary nature of the pact.
Mexican labor was not to displace United States labor. Guarantees appeared governing wages, transportation of workers to
and from their homes, and the right of either government to
terminate the agreement with ninety days' notice.

Within a year some modifications in the agreement
occurred. The United States Congress, ever responsive to political pressure, reacted to grower discontent with the excessive
protections built into the executive agreement of the previous
year. Public Law 45, passed in April, 1943, gave the executive
branch authority to use public monies for the operation of the
program. Thus, the Department of Agriculture assumed administrative jurisdiction over the bracero program. Within the
USDA different agencies assumed responsibility for the program but were often susceptible to grower and farmer pressures. While exploitation continued to occur, this was limited
by law.

In general, the wartime bracero program allowed the production of agricultural products for an economy besieged by
war. Braceros took up the slack in agricultural labor and provided the necessary work to avert even greater food shortages
than did exist in the period 1942-1954. The program, while
expensive for the United States ($113 million), provided the
needed labor plus guarantees of medical expenses, transportation, subsistence while traveling, and minimum education for
workers that ultimately benefitted Mexico after the war.

The bulk of bracero labor went into United States agriculture. Yet, some were diverted to industry, especially in railroads after 1941. Originally opposed by the railway union, the use of Mexican labor on track crews and later in other phases of railroad work proved a necessity with the onset of war. As war came to a close in 1945, the railways became accustomed to bracero labor and wanted an extension of the program. The request was denied, and braceros working on the railroads were sent home by April 1946.

While Mexico and the United States generally derived mutual benefits from the bracero program, Texas remained aloof from participation. Texas had long been an advocate of an open border policy for immigrant labor and strove to attain that end. Such an end contradicted the Mexican-United States agreement, but in May, 1943, the U.S. Department of Immigration acceded to Texas demands for workers bearing one-year immigrant laborer cards. Mexico's government growled a lot about the exception, and the United States quickly rescinded the permission. In June, 1943, the Mexican Secretariat of Foreign Relations announced that no workers from Mexico would be allowed to go into Texas because of the constant complaints about discrimination against Mexicans in that state.

Texas felt the squeeze. Its legislature passed an act that provided for no discrimination in public places, and the governor of Texas informed the Mexican government of the act. However, Foreign Minister Ezequiel Padilla wrote off the action as tokenism, and no Mexican laborers entered Texas for the remainder of 1943. The two remaining years of the war saw Mexico still reluctant to send braceros to Texas. As a consequence, Texas was forced to use prisoners of war, Mexican-Americans, school children, and college students to fill needed seasonal labor jobs.

The bracero void in Texas proved beneficial to Mexican-American workers in the state. Legislation provided for better working conditions as an inducement for domestic labor to take up the slack. In one respect, the Texas experience could be seen as a forerunner of some of the problems that emerged in the 1960s revolving around agricultural labor and the concomitant emergence of Chicano militancy.

In general, the bracero program received a good press on both sides of the Río Grande. Mexicans coming to the United States emerged from varied backgrounds but generally fared better economically than did their counter-parts remaining in Mexico. Growers obtained the needed labor for the continued production of crops. Growers also benefitted from experienced labor after the first year of the program. Because of underemployment and general economic dislocation in Mexico most braceros wanted to return to the United States. Thus, returnees constituted nearly 70 percent of the bracero work force by 1945. This, in turn, reenforced a *patrón-peón* relationship, and growers began to think more and more in terms of "their Mexicans."

The bracero program during the war period constituted an attempt to solve a labor shortage, and in one respect it provided for exploitation of imported workers. Discrimination existed; wages were held down through either governmental action or private action among growers; housing and food were substandard in some instances; and working conditions in the fields—including exposure to strong pesticides—made the braceros lot less than Elysian. Still, the program was continued by mutual agreement between Mexico and the United States in 1947.

The war period caused tension and dislocation between some Chicanos and the dominant Anglo. Mexican-American communities throughout California and the Southwest proudly displayed blue stars for members of families serving in the Armed Forces. These often were replaced by gold stars symbolizing those killed in action. Mexican-Americans did not experience the high degree of exemption as a result of selective service regulations, but they served without complaint. Some of those that stayed home, however, demonstrated the obverse side of the Chicano coin. While brothers, cousins, fathers, and uncles risked their brown hides in Europe and the Pacific, snotty-nosed younger relatives proceeded to raise merry hell and to affect outlandish outfits and behavior.

Prior to World War II, most Mexican-American communities were essentially segregated and suffered from social and economic discrimination. The war loosened the traditional restraints. Pachucos or Mexican-American youths between the ages of 13 and 17 began to dress in garish clothes in an attempt to achieve some sort of identity. In the barrios they formed gangs or *palomillas* composed of members from the same barrios. To claim distinction for these herds of recalcitrant adolescents is an absurdity. Similar developments occurred in most big cities among Blacks, Puerto Ricans, Italians, Poles, or hodgepodge whites. Such action might be more the result of poverty and the general peer groupiness of adolescence than some unique manifestation of Chicano culture.

One recent general study of the Chicano attributes the emergence of the pachuco as an attempt by a hybridized culture to strive for separateness from the dominant Anglo culture. The prominent Mexican poet and essayist, Octavio Paz, states that "instead of attempting a problematical adjustment to society, the pachuco actually flaunts his differences. The purpose of his grotesque dandyism and anarchic behavior is not so much to point out the injustice and incapacity of a society that has failed to assimilate him as it is to demonstrate his personal will to remain different."* Thus, the pachucos provide an historic antecedent to the Brown Berets and other Chicano resistance groups.

Alienation existed, of that there is no doubt. That the pachucos felt any more alienated than similar gangs in Anglo neighborhoods is more difficult to ascertain. In part the sense

---

*As cited in Rodolfo Acuña. *Occupied America: The Chicano Struggle for Liberation* (San Francisco: Canfield Press, 1972), p. 201.

of separateness was undoubtedly the result of general bias felt against Mexican-Americans. Consequently, these youngsters, in asserting their inexorable adolescence like other kids their age, unknowingly added to it some degree of *Kulturkampf*.

During the war years, the pachuco phenomenon and its attendant social tension erupted into incidents of violence, especially in Los Angeles County. Here approximately 10 percent of the population was Mexican-American, concentrated primarily in East Lost Angeles and smaller Mexican enclaves throughout the county. As war drained the United States of its young men between the ages of 17 and 30—many of whom were Mexican-Americans—the young pachucos in the barrios saw here an opportunity to assert their machismo, to attain some of the masculinity that resulted from service in the Armed Forces. Such assertion came into direct conflict with growing antiforeignism on the part of the Anglos. Anti-Japanese and anti-German sentiments ran high, and these expanded into near xenophobia during the war. The Mexican-American, unfortunately and despite his distinguished record in the Armed Forces, became the object of nativist elements in Los Angeles County.

Tensions began to build up in 1942 and erupted in the Sleepy Lagoon Case. On August 1, 1942, Sleepy Lagoon, located in the Mexican-American area of Los Angeles, became the spot for one hell of a party. Lots of booze flowed, and inter-*palomilla* tensions rose to the surface. One gang, the 38th Street gang, arrived at the party searching for someone that had beaten up one of their members. The next day, a Chicano by the name of José Díaz was found dead. The police arrested the entire 38th Street Gang, the newspapers had a field day, and a Grand Jury had a case revolving around criminal conspiracy to commit murder.

The Grand Jury functioned in a charged atmosphere. The recurrent accounts of pachuco activities plus the unnecessary sensationalism of the Los Angeles press conditioned the Grand Jury to assume an anti-Mexican posture. In addition, the head of the Foreign Relations Bureau of the Los Angeles Police Department submitted a report to the Grand Jury that depicted the Mexican as innately cruel and possessing a total indifference toward human life. The more comical aspect of the report attributed Mexican cruelty to the fact that Mexicans were descended from the Aztecs, and these dudes committed countless human sacrifices.

As the trial lapsed into the end of 1942, the courtroom took on a more prejudiced view. The presiding judge committed some major magisterial blunders. The prosecution apparently could not prove its case conclusively. Yet, in January, 1943, the twenty-two defendants were found guilty of crimes ranging from conspiracy to murder in the first degree.

Into the breach stepped the enraged liberal elements of Los Angeles County. Headed by Carey McWilliams, the Sleepy Lagoon Defense Committee set out to prove that the *pachuquitos* ("little pachucos") had been framed. The committee was Red baited, investigated, and generally harassed. Yet, they did prove successful. In October, 1944, the Second District Court of Appeals unanimously held that the defendants in the Sleepy Lagoon Case had been handled in a prejudicial manner, that their constitutional rights had been violated, and that no evidence existed that linked the 38th Street Gang with the death of José Díaz.

Baiting of the Sleepy Lagoon Defense Committee began to manifest itself in increased Anglo antagonism toward the Mexican-American in East Los Angeles. The Committee, in its defense of the 38th Street Gang, touched a raw nerve among the nativists who saw in the Mexican-American a real threat to Anglo purity. Beginning in June, 1943, while the Defense Committee worked to build up the appeal for the 38th Street Gang, East Los Angeles became the scene for conflict. Police arrests of Mexican-Americans, primarily for burglary, the establishment of road blocks, and peremptory search of Mexican-Americans for suspicion of larceny received massive headlines in the Los Angeles press and excited racial/ethnic tensions.

The situation became increasingly complicated as service-men, mainly sailors, arrived at Long Beach and San Pedro on short furloughs looking for a good time. They went into Los Angeles, attempted to pick up Mexican-American girls that reminded them of hookers in Tijuana, Baja California, and generally conducted themselves like servicemen anywhere during wartime. As a result, pachucos grew increasingly pro-tective about their pachucas, and small fights erupted through-out the spring of 1943. The pachuco, asserting his macho pre-rogative over his female counterpart, collided with the sailors, most of them young, who also wanted to assert their mascu-linity. Alleged brutality by Mexican-Americans brought swift retaliation by sailors and marines. Greaser stomping became something of a pastime.

By June, 1943, the stage was set for all hell to break loose. Sailors and pachucos clashed. Sailors broke into the Carmen Theater, ripped zoot-suits off pachucos, beat the Mexican-Americans, and got out before the police arrived. Pachucos were arrested for starting a riot. On June 4, another bunch of sailors returned and began a systematic rampage in East Los Angeles. The Los Angeles press, joyous over the sensational goings-on, built up the conflicts between servicemen and pachucos. Throughout the early part of June, 1943, service-men and pachucos were at war. All Mexicans became suspect and ready targets for retaliation.

Ultimately, what helped cool things down in East Los Angeles was the Government of Mexico. Mexican officials were dismayed over the apparent racism in the riots. The United States Government, in turn, feared that the bracero agreement might suffer abrogation if things failed to calm. Pressure was applied to California generally and Los Angeles County specifically to clean up the mess. Committees were formed, officials declared that steps were being taken to eradicate injustice, and Los Angeles County officials began to take a hard line toward all disrupters of public order.

The pachuco riots caused polarity between Anglos and Mexican-Americans and within the Mexican-American community itself. *Gente decente* ("decent people") in the barrio refused to be identified with the pachucos, for they considered these the same as the scummy *pelados* ("ragged fellows") from Mexico. Already could be seen the conflict that would make itself apparent in the 1960s: namely, the divisions within the Mexican-American community between those that chose chauvinistic separatism and those that opted for practical assimilation.

Another by-product of the 1930s that affected the Mexican-American was *sinarquismo*, imported from Mexico by local Mexican-Americans. This philosophy emphasized strong Mexican nationalism, corporate statism, and a resurgence of religious fervor as opposed to the anticlerical, reform-oriented programs of the Mexican government. For the Mexican-Americans, the *sinarquista* philosophy held some appeal. It favored the return of the Southwest to Mexico and pressed Mexican-Americans to withhold support from the war effort after 1941. Despite claims by the *sinarquistas* in the Southwest, the membership was never large, and the influence of the group declined even more as the war opened economic opportunities for the Mexican-Americans.

New economic avenues for Mexican-Americans introduced new life-styles. Urban, industrial patterns developed. Mexican-American women left the home to seek employment in defense industries. Rosita the Riveter joined her Anglo sister Rosie in augmenting family incomes and supporting the war effort. Increased defense research and the concomitant expenditures by federal agencies opened more opportunities for Mexican-Americans. The Manhattan Project for the development of the atomic bomb increased employment for Mexican-Americans in New Mexico. Research facilities at Los Alamos, Alamogordo, and White Sands offered high-paying jobs for Mexican-Americans.

In consequence of these shifts in occupational and social patterns among Mexican-Americans, the New Mexico Department of Vocational Education increased its activities in training Hispanos. Hispanos obtained jobs in highly skilled industrial areas throughout the Southwest and California. In Texas, the wartime expansion of the oil industry again provided more jobs for Mexican-Americans. Meat packing also opened opportunities. In Texas, discrimination did exist. Distinguished Mexican-American scholars like George I. Sánchez and Carlos Castañeda of the University of Texas headed committees to assure that the Fair Employment Practices Act was adhered to by employers. Sánchez pressed for bilingual education for Mexican-American children in order for them to take advantage of the new opportunities that would eventually come their way. Toward this end, attempts were also made to end discrimination in the public schools of Texas and to foster an understanding of Mexican and Latin American history and culture through teacher-training workshops.

Termination of hostilities with victory over Japan in August, 1945, and the slow return of veterans to the United States provided Mexican-American GIs with increased opportunities. The GI Bill offered chances for vocational training, increased education, and real estate loans that had not been available to Mexican-Americans before. Some Mexican-Americans went to school, others started businesses, and some bought new homes. These Mexican-American veterans broke down some of the Mexican-American provinciality that had characterized them before their full participation in the war effort. They became aware of chances to improve their social and economic status.

The return of Mexican-American veterans did not instantly improve their status at home. The larger society, conditioned by pachuco riots and the Sleepy Lagoon caper, remained suspicious of the Mexican-American, especially those seasoned in combat. As a result, groups began to form that

were oriented toward Mexican-American attainment of full
civil rights. In the immediate post-war period, social, political,
and service organizations such as the Mexican American
Political Association, the American GI Forum, and the Political Association of Spanish-Speaking Organizations joined the
League of United Latin American Citizens (LULAC) in attempting to organize the Mexican-American and to assimilate
him into the larger society.

While World War II served as an impetus for the
formation of organizations for Mexican-Americans, this in itself was not unique. World War I also gave rise to Mexican-
American societies aimed at procuring more rights for
Mexican-American citizens. Disparate organizations sprang up
throughout the 1920s. In 1929, however, a coalition of different organizations formed the League of United Latin American Citizens in Corpus Christi, Texas. When the first general
meeting of the new organization convened in May, 1929, its
constitution clearly stated the aims of the group. It stressed the
attainment of political, economic, and social equality for
Mexican-Americans. It also proclaimed as a major objective
the encouragement of more Mexican-Americans in the professions. Moreover, while stressing bilingualism, LULAC aimed
at the promotion of pride in the Mexican heritage. Finally, it
sought to encourage Mexican-Americans to exercise their full
political rights and to participate actively in politics at all
levels.

Thus, LULAC spread rather rapidly. Its ranks swelled as
chapters grew in Arizona, New Mexico, and California, thus
augmenting the Texas core. LULAC chapters also grew in
large urban areas outside of the Southwest and California and
included a chapter in Washington, D.C. By 1945, LULAC
claimed two hundred local councils with a membership of approximately 15,000. In the immediate post-war epoch LULAC
stressed educational objectives and strove to end discrimination in the schools. In Texas and California LULAC succeeded

in the elimination of de facto segregation, and in New Mexico LULAC helped win a case that ended job discrimination in 1949.

The early formation of LULAC and the subsequent growth of other organizations after 1945 underscored one of the weaknesses of the Mexican-American community. The fierce individuality of the Mexican-American, a heritage directly traceable to Mexican and Spanish antecedents, did not allow for cooperation between different groups with similar objectives but with different egos involved. As a result, the Mexican-American community, rather than maintaining a cohesive front, has instead divided along personal and socio-economic lines. In addition, the composition of the different groups essentially emphasized the upwardly mobile nature of most of the Mexican-Americans that returned home from the war. No longer were they content to sit by in their provincialism. Instead, they sought practical assimilation and acquired middle- and upper-class attitudes. This, of course, still left a number of Mexican-Americans, both urban and rural, outside of the struggle for material goodies.

The bracero arrangement between Mexico and the United States expired in 1947. No longer were Mexican laborers necessary to fill jobs in agriculture and industry because the GIs were home. Yet, United States growers were loathe to give up the cheap and experienced labor. Returning GIs, fat with the GI Bill, disdained the menial labor of the fields and sought to improve their status through varied educational programs. As a consequence the agricultural jobs still remained unfilled, and American agriculturalists found themselves in the same box of burgeoning crops and no one to pick them. While termination of the program did not stop the flow of legal migrants into the United States, it became the responsibility of farmers' associations to make the most of the arrangements with the governments of Mexico and the United States.

Pressure for a more regularized flow of migrant labor

forced the United States and Mexico to enter into another labor agreement in February, 1948. This agreement, however, did not contain the numerous guarantees for the workers that appeared in the earlier accord. Substandard wages in the spring and fall of 1948 forced the Mexican government to insist that the going wage rate be paid to Mexican laborers. When growers refused, the flow of Mexican labor to the United States ceased. However, the Immigration Service came to the rescue of cotton growers in Texas. They were told that the crop would rot in the fields unless some labor were allowed into the area to pick the cotton. Thus, from October 13 to 18 the Texas border became an open sesame for Mexican workers choosing to come to the United States of their own volition. Approximately 7,000 Mexicans crossed into the United States, were arrested for illegal entry, and conveniently paroled to the U.S. Employment Service for shipment to various cotton centers. Mexican protests resulted in no action from the United States, at least until the cotton crop was saved. Consequently, Mexico abrogated the February, 1948 migrant labor agreement.

For nine months no agreement existed between Mexico and the United States about immigrant labor. Increase in illegal immigrant labor marked the period, and both governments sought to alleviate the situation. In August, 1949, a new accord was reached that stressed a suppression of wetback, or *mojado*, labor and the denial of braceros to those farmers using illegal immigrants. At the same time a provision was made for the legalization of those wetbacks already in the United States. Of course violations of contracts still occurred, and the Mexican government seemed displeased with the arrangement.

Throughout the rest of the 1940s recurrent problems arose with Mexican labor. The outbreak of war (pardon me, police action) in Korea in 1950 gave the Mexican government the necessary clout to force a stricter control agreement out of the United States. Mexico declared emphatically that if the United

States wanted laborers it would have to revert to the guarantees for braceros under the old Public Law 45 of World War II. A presidential commission made a study of the problem, made its recommendation to President Harry S. Truman, and on July 12, 1951, a Migratory Labor Agreement was signed. Thus, Public Law 78 was passed by the Congress as a two-year temporary measure during the war. Public Law 78 made the Department of Labor the responsible agency for the new bracero program. Braceros would be contracted for periods ranging from six weeks to six months with guarantees of work for at least 75 percent of the time in the United States and were to receive the prevailing wage as established by the Secretary of Labor.

Meanwhile, the problem of illegal immigrant labor into the United States from Mexico did not abate with the new agreement. Instead, there was an increase in wetback labor. Yet, there was historic precedent for the flow of labor into the United States. Throughout the nineteenth century the immigrant flow from Mexico was virtually unhindered. Only with the 1910 Revolution and the subsequent violence did restrictions become necessary. These carried on into the 1920s. Thus, as. Mexican-Americans moved out of agricultural regions in the Southwest, they were replaced by *mojado* labor.

For the grower, wetback labor was a blessing. No real penalties existed for the use of illegal labor. Such labor would work for wretched wages and living conditions that seemed, at first glance, an improvement over the situation in Mexico. In the 1950s "Operation Wetback" aimed at rounding up illegal immigrants and shipping them back to Mexico. This still did not stop the wetback flow. Between 1950 and 1955 over 3 million wetbacks were deported, but the brown flood continued.

The wetback roundup had some positive as well as negative aspects. For one thing, it removed illegal immigrants from jobs that could be had by Mexican-Americans. Thus, the labor supply was minimized and wages could go up. But there was another side to the question. Many of the migrants had families. These were broken up by the Immigration Service when the head of the family was shipped back to Mexico, and the women and children became burdens on the general society. Many wives and children, most of them United States citizens, went to Mexico rather than be separated from husbands and fathers. As a result, many Mexican-American families felt a gnawing distrust of government officialdom because of the legal but calloused deportations of the 1950s.

For the Mexican-American, the *mojados* provided an ambiguity. They depressed wages; they retarded the acceptance of the Mexican-American by the Anglo; but, By God! they were members of *la raza*. Here was cultural reenforcement of the first water. Language, folk ideas, communal cohesiveness tended to be underscored by the illegal immigrants. Their deportation affected the stability of many Mexican-American communities and caused social and cultural dislocations.

Unfortunately, Public Law 78 failed to stem the flow of *mojados* into the United States. The agreements between Mexico and the United States were renewed in 1954, 1956, and 1958, kept viable by a Congresssional coalition of Republicans and southern Democrats who represented agricultural interests. Finally, in 1964, the bracero program was officially terminated. Criticism and controversy surrounded the program during its entire lifetime. It was opposed by organized labor and supported by agribusiness interests. Pressures from Mexican-Americans also hastened the demise of the bracero program, for the braceros constituted a threat to the economic symbiosis of the agricultural areas.

For those Mexican-Americans unaffected by the GI Bill and by the greater social mobility of the post-war period, some organizations filled the void for the disaffected. Many Mexican-Americans did not "dig" the GI Forum or LULAC, for all of these were essentially middle-class and assimilation-

oriented. United Leagues were formed outside of the greater
Los Angeles area, for example. Their principal instigator was
Ignacio López, editor of *El Espectador*. Assisting López was
Fred Ross, an associate of the notorious (depending on your
point of view) Saul Alinsky.

The United Leagues followed the Alinsky dictum of
letting the Establishment commit an error and then capital-
izing on that error in order to precipitate a crisis. Its principal
tactic was one of confrontation with nonnegotiable demands.
From the Unity Leagues grew the Community Service Organization (CSO). These were organized principally by middle-
class Mexican-Americans. The CSO, while initially nonpol-
itical, registered sufficient Mexican-American voters to assure
the election of Edward Roybal to the City Council in Los
Angeles in 1949. Up to the present, the CSO works essentially
in rural areas and is nominally non-political. One recent study
of the Mexican-American criticizes the CSO chapter in Delano
for not supporting the farm workers, and condemns it instead
for working "in collusion with the Anglo establishment
there."*

Throughout the above mentioned work there exists a
subtle condemnation of these Mexican-Americans who opted
for assimilation and for cooperation with the dominant culture. By some strange definition these poor benighted devils
aren't even Mexicans anymore. They are, in effect, Oreo
cookies: brown on the outside but white on the inside. Such an
approach to the Mexican-American is sheer claptrap, but this
is the sort of thing that is being perpetrated by "Chicano"
quasi scholars fraught with their own ethnic hang-ups. These
we shall deal with in a later chapter.

The 1950s were an age of Senator Joseph McCarthy and a
bunch of other nativists who stressed Anglo purity and a
stultifying conformism. Legislation, namely the McCarran-
Walter Immigration Act of 1952, complicated some of the

---

*Acuña, *Occupied America*, p. 210.

naturalization procedures and provided for denaturalization and deportation of undesirables. Yet, with the conclusion of the Korean Police Action more Mexican-Americans took advantage of the GI Bill and furthered their education and social mobility.

Throughout the 1940s and 1950s, Mexican-Americans received opportunities for education and advancement that previously had been denied them either de facto or through intent. The war opened industrial jobs for Mexican-Americans who left the fields for the factories. At the same time braceros and illegal immigrants filled agricultural jobs. Of course with the termination of hostilities some problems existed, and it was not until 1964 that the bracero program was eliminated. Yet, the broadened horizons of most Mexican-Americans allowed them to break a provincial pattern and at the same time attain greater material goods and social status. For those that saw such action as selling out to The Man, the Alinsky breed of organization gave them an outlet for their frustrated separatism. This sort of inwardly directed chauvinism would preoccupy much of the 1960s.

Part II

Nonsense, dear, we need Mexico
economically speaking — where else
would we get Tequila from?

Introduction

The arrival of the Mexican-American to the decade of the 1960s found him prepared for a variety of courses in order to assure his share of the American dream. The Camelot-like atmosphere of the Kennedy years (1961-1963) created among Mexican-Americans a desire and later a demand for President John F. Kennedy to make good upon campaign promises to better the lot of minorities in the United States. Instead of action, however, the Mexican-Americans found that the promises were mere political rhetoric and the action miniscule tokenism.

For those Mexican-Americans at the bottom of the social totem pole the Kennedy brouhaha proved a bitter disillusionment. Instead of improved wages, working conditions, and status they were again patently ignored by yet another Anglo politician who had manipulated them for electoral purposes. If they were going to be ripped off, some Mexican-Americans turned to more militant forms of expression to voice their disenchantment with the Anglo machinery and the Anglo society.

95

It is during the 1960s that the Mexican-American nationalists become articulate. Some, like Corky González and his Crusade for Justice in Denver, Colorado, sought cultural and political roots in Mexican tradition. César Estrada Chávez and his grape strikers sought to use Anglo unions as a means of achieving parity with Anglos. Reies López Tijerina and his *Alianza Federal de los Pueblos Libres* delved into Spanish land laws to justify their claims to lands in New Mexico.

Generally, the Mexican-American in the 1960s demonstrated the same lack of cohesion that in previous decades prevented any type of unified action. Traditional forces, generally found in the folk culture of Mexico, worked more pervasively than did the immediate social and economic aspirations prattled by demagogues and politicians. It was, in fact, this traditional hold that forced Mexican-Americans into a distorted hunt for "true" roots and "true" identity.

Emergence of Chicano studies programs, especially in the Far West and the Southwest, became academic manifestations of the Chicano desire to understand himself as an integral being. These, unfortunately, became soapboxes for political and academic opportunists, Anglo and Chicano, who sought to manipulate the Mexican-American to their own ends. Thus, diversity and individualism, both the blessing and the curse of the Mexican-American, continued to dominate any attempts to achieve Chicano unity. The more vocal one became throughout the 1960s, the more attention he received. Thus, a majority often was measured more in decibels than in individual head counts. As a result, the Mexican-American continued in his own varied ways with the vocal ones receiving the attention.

While necessity dictates that we deal with Chicano noisemakers in this section, it should be noted that the Mexican-American who is merely "doing his own thing" is not very well represented. Why? Simply because he is too busy to become excessively involved in divisiveness and dissension, two things that would detract from the search for his individual aspiration.

6

Grapes and Turf:
La Huelga
and the
Land Grant Dispute

In all probability the greatest impact upon the Mexican-American came in the 1960s. At a time when students were revolting (both literally and figuratively), when Black militants screamed "Burn, baby, burn!," and a general disintegration of values within the social fabric occurred, Mexican-Americans, or, according to some, Chicanos, viewed the turmoil as an opportunity to cash in on a good thing. Two major areas of concern occupied the minds of Chicano leaders: the alleged rip-off of grape workers in California; and the reduction of Hispano lands in New Mexico.

Both issues, erupting in the mid 1960s, became causes célèbres of politicians who hoped to capitalize upon their acquaintance with the leaders of the two distinct movements. Both movements began as specific disputes with limited objectives and were eventually generalized into major facets of a burgeoning Chicano movement. As a result, greater pressure was exerted upon Mexican-Americans to sympathize with the struggle of their *carnales* ("soul brothers") in California and New Mexico. The disputes in these two states thus became focal points of supposed unity among all Mexican-Americans whether they wanted it or not.

Chronologically, the first of the movements to attract major attention occurred in Delano, California, a small town whose stable population was comprised of merchants, field workers, growers, and the ancillary enterprises that go along with agriculture. As a town Delano is not particularly attractive. It did, however, afford full employment to the field workers who lived there, owned homes, purchased goods and food stuffs in the town, and sent their children to Delano schools that were supported, in part, by field worker property taxes. Yet, this became the principal target for the National Farm Workers Association (NFWA) headed by César Estrada Chávez, the enigmatic and charismatic figure that would be catapulted into national attention by a strike against the table grape industry centered in Delano.

Much has been written about César Chávez as the son of a migrant family, struggling to grow up in San Jose, California, becoming aware of the terrible inequities that afflicted rural labor and especially the Mexican-American. Also, Chávez has been depicted as an almost Gandhiesque character, loving his fellow man, eschewing violence, calling for peaceful resolution of human problems. His detractors view him as a conniving labor czar who deliberately defrauded the grape pickers in order to aggrandize his labor union.* Generally, this latter view seems more accurate and to the point, for it dwells on the ability of one man to manipulate others and to use what can best be described as shady tactics to achieve his ends. In many respects, however, César Chávez merits consideration, for he was able to force through unionization in the grape fields of Delano without even holding a collective bargaining election, no mean feat if the laws are strictly observed.

Chávez became a devotee of Fred Ross, a chief honcho in the CSO. Chávez became an organizer for Ross and traveled throughout California, establishing CSO chapters and getting a feel for the job that needed to be done. Ostensibly in his travels Chávez grew increasingly appalled by the dreadful conditions of agricultural workers. In 1962, Chávez resigned from the CSO in order to devote himself entirely to organizing agricultural workers in California. He moved his family to Delano and began organizing the National Farm Workers Association.

When Chávez and his union were ready to go, they discovered that the Agricultural Workers Organizing Committee (AWOC), an AFL-CIO affiliate, in Delano, led by the Filipino Larry Itliong, voted to strike against the Di Giorgio Corporation, one of the largest of the grape growers. In September, 1965, the NFWA voted to support the AWOC move, fearful that the NFWA would lose the march to the Filipinos.

From the outset the strike depended upon outside support. Massive walkouts of field workers failed to occur. Chávez, to some observers, seemed a leader without a following. As a consequence, he called in outsiders to help break the back of Di Giorgio and other growers in the Delano area. College students, civil rights militants, union organizers, untheological clerics of every stripe came to Delano to support the strike against the pernicious growers. Picket lines went up around

---

*Much of this chapter is based on Ralph de Toledano, *Little César* (Anthem Books, 1971).

the fields. Bull horns wielded by some of Chávez' outside help-
ers roared to workers to join *la huelga*. Women working in the
fields were subjected to obscenities, and more than once *puta*
("whore") and *hija de la chingada* ("daughter of a bitch") ac-
costed the ears of women workers.

When Chávez began his union organizing in 1962 he concentrated primarily upon the Mexican-American workers. He
appealed to a sense of nationalism and ethnic pride. This,
however, did not garner full-scale support for his efforts. His
union dues in 1962 were $3.50 per month, a high rate for lower
income families. In addition, by 1964, Chávez could claim that
the union was self-supporting, for he avoided entanglements
until such a time as he could build an effective power base and
move quickly against a single target.

Before that fateful day in Delano when Chávez chose to
support Itliong, the NFWA became painfully aware of the deficiency in its ranks: members. Consequently, the call went
out. Civil rights workers, socially activist clergy, college students out on a lark came to Delano, became union members,
and joined the pickets. Many idealistic people—some of them
of the radical chic variety—joined the allegedly Gandhi-like
Chávez because of his espousal of nonviolence.

When the strike began in September, 1965, most workers
on the Di Giorgio farms chose to remain on their jobs. Yet, the
propaganda machine generated by César Chávez claimed that
thousands had gone off the job and that the growers were using
immigrants and scab labor to bring in the crops. Pressures
were brought to bear on other unions, notably the Teamsters.
In 1966, the Teamsters, who before had rejected overtures from
Chávez, refused to cross picket lines in San Francisco. Rumors
of a bartenders' strike also reached the Schenley Corporation,
and they signed a contract with NFWA. Soon other major
wineries in California followed suit. This left only the intransigent Di Giorgio corporation.

The new corporation president, Robert Di Giorgio, was
well trained in public relations and sought to counter the

Chávez propaganda with a little action of his own. In April, 1966, he announced that he would allow the workers at the company's Sierra Vista ranch to hold a collective bargaining election. If the NFWA won the election, it would then be the official bargaining agent for the workers, and Di Giorgio would be forced to negotiate with them. Yet a fly crept into the ointment. The NFWA dragged its feet on the election. Instead, it wanted Di Giorgio to recognize them unilaterally without the benefit of an election. From April to June, 1966, Chávez and his group played fickle whore with Di Giorgio.

The Teamsters, in addition, turned on Chávez and petitioned to be allowed on the ballot as contenders for the bargaining agency. The Di Giorgio Corporation called the election, Chávez refused to participate on the grounds that the NFWA had not been consulted as to procedures and date, and of the 385 workers voting, the Teamsters received 281 votes. César and company screamed fraud, and demanded that Governor Edmund G. "Pat" Brown call an investigation of the rigged proceedings. Brown, needing agribusiness support but also needing the backing of liberals throughout California, sent an investigator to Delano. He declared that the election was irregular and set a new date of August 30, 1966, for another election.

Throughout the summer of 1966 NFWA campaigned vigorously to become the bargaining agent for the workers vis-à-vis the Di Giorgios. Chávez faced a plethora of problems, not the least of which included feeding his supporters who joined the strike. The union was broke; pressure on Chávez to merge with AWOC increased. Chávez, sacrificing his avowed independence, finally joined with Larry Itliong and as a consequence became a part of the massive AFL-CIO machinery. The new United Farm Workers Organizing Committee (UFWOC) now had the monetary clout to give the growers a thorough drubbing. Some of Chávez' more idealistic supporters thought that he had sold out his moral independence.

The campaign intensified in the last weeks before the

election. Violent propaganda charges flew back and forth. UFWOC distributed literature regarding the corruption of the Teamsters' leadership. The Teamsters, in turn, accused the UFWOC of communist affiliation. Finally, the election came. Imported union members swelled the small ranks of Chávez' local organization, and the UFWOC won the election 573 to 425 for the Teamsters. Di Giorgio was forced to negotiate a contract with UFWOC.

Yet, Chávez remained unsatisfied. Other growers did not yield as readily to his pressures. In 1967, Chávez aimed at the Giumarra Vineyards, probably the largest of the table grape producers. By this time Chávez began an extensive boycott operation aimed at bringing the growers to their knees. Stores throughout the nation were urged not to stock grapes that did not bear the UFWOC label, a stylized black Aztec eagle. Giumarra circumvented the boycott by using labels belonging to other companies that had been pressured by Chávez into signing with his union. As a consequence, Chávez extended his boycott to all table grapes from California. Grape sales decreased, but the Department of Defense purchased surplus grapes to send to United States forces in Viet Nam. By 1969, the Defense Department purchased 4 million pounds of table grapes to send to Southeast Asia. The Defense Department also purchased lettuce produced by growers struck by UFWOC.

Then Chávez turned to the lettuce fields of the Salinas Valley. Again, student groups and the boycott became the weapon. This time, however, Chávez was forced to compromise with the Teamsters. A negotiated settlement between UFWOC and the Teamsters gave jurisdiction of field workers to the former and the food processors to the latter. By 1971, Chávez and the Teamsters moved to strangle the lettuce industry of California. Injunctions against Chávez and his short incarceration in December, 1970, failed to stop his forward momentum. Instead, it gave Chávez a publicity advantage. He claimed persecution by the industrial giants and received the support of the radical chic elements of the nation.

Since 1971, Chávez and company have encountered difficulties with their erstwhile allies, the Teamsters. Teamster organizational efforts after 1971 began to break the Chávez' hold
on field workers. Growers began signing "sweetheart" contracts with Teamster locals as a means of alleviating the hold
that César Chávez had over them. By May, 1975, Chávez and
the Teamsters broke violently. By now the United Farm
Workers and the Teamsters clashed in Sacramento while both
picketed the state government for support in their attempts to
control California agriculture. In that same month, California
Governor Gerry Brown, son of "Pat" Brown, showed more
guts that did his father. At the end of May he signed a bill into
law that provided for secret elections for collective bargaining
agents in California agriculture.

The phenomenon of César Chávez, labor leader from San
Jose who emerged as the principal exponent of a closed shop
in agriculture, ties in inextricably with the cultural roots of the
Mexican-American. Chávez' appeal to his followers resided
primarily in his charisma, a certain magnetism, that virtually
forced his disciples to forgive him his indiscretions and pre-
varications. He played the news media and the liberal community, especially academicians, like classical Bach. The
counterpoint of humility and quiet strength that Chávez pro-
jected served him well among his less analytical admirers.

A series of events—culminating in his penitential fast—
illustrate the Chávez phenomenon. According to Chávez, in
March, 1966, he and his union workers decided to march on
Sacramento to underscore the plight of the farm workers. On
March 16, he informed the police department of Delano that he
intended to lead a march beginning in Delano and culminating in Sacramento. The Delano police chief informed
Don César that he needed a parade permit in order to have a
march. Unfortunately, Chávez did not have time to procure the
permit and was told instead that he should have his people

walk on the sidewalks rather than down the middle of the street. In this way the law would remain inviolate, and Chávez could have his peaceful demonstration.

The next day about sixty people gathered outside the union headquarters—the Forty Acres—and were accompanied by newspaper and television representatives. The police department of Delano recognized instantly that Chávez wanted the demonstration disbanded by the brutal police force. Television cameras stood in readiness, waiting to capture yet another incident of praetorianism being used against a helpless people. Yet the marchers were not disbanded; instead, Chávez and his crew were forced to make the long march to Sacramento, something for which they were woefully unprepared. Chávez and his followers found themselves between a rock and a hard spot. They sent out the call for assistance. Students again volunteered, furry-brained liberals marched with the strikers for a day or two, and by the time the march reached Sacramento on April 10, the vast majority of the original contingent were nowhere in evidence. Chávez' intention was obvious. He wrapped his cause in the banner of the Virgin of Guadalupe and posited the march as a symbolic gathering of the Mexican-American people. Chávez frankly cared little about the impact of the march on Delano, the pickers, and the growers. His audience was the world outside of the San Joaquín Valley, including Governor Brown and the political clout of the United States Congress.

The attendant publicity brought additional pressure on Schenley, Incorporated. Pickets in Chicago, New York, Detroit, and other large metropolitan areas of the country surrounded liquor stores that handled Schenley products. Finally, in the midst of the march, Schenley agreed to sign a union contract. A major victory had been won by Chávez. Unfortunately, when the NFWA failed to produce the requisite workers for the harvest, Schenley plowed under its crops and robbed many workers of jobs they had held in the past.

The march on Sacramento represented but one of many

attempts to garner support for the starving farm workers of
Delano. The piéce de résistance, however, came on February
19, 1968. Chávez assembled his sycophants and supporters and
proceeded to give them merry hell about the excesses of violence that had crept into *la causa*. He harangued them at
length, and then César announced that he would fast as atone-
ment for the sins of his followers. With that, he marched off to
union headquarters at the Forty Acres.

Chávez' hangers-on established a shrine outside union
headquarters. The secret fast that César announced became
public knowledge through well-placed leaks in the press.
Senator Robert Kennedy wired his support. Chávez' fashion-
able supporters twittered about the penitential sacrifice in
which César was engaged. Surprisingly, his spiritual food
must have contained a substantial number of calories. During
the two months of the fast César failed to lose weight. One
Chávez detractor reported that Chávez' wife made trips to a
local restaurant for a supply of strawberry milkshakes and
grilled sandwiches, César's favorite restaurant fare. These
would then be carried in a bag to the Forty Acres. In addition,
the doctor who examined Chávez after the fast noted no
physiological changes typical of a body that underwent nu-
tritional privation.

The full force of Chávez' fast made itself apparent when
Senator Robert Kennedy rushed to Delano to be with Chávez
when the Great One decided to get back to solid foods. At the
request of a TV cameraman, Kennedy fed Chávez his "first"
piece of bread in over a month. One picture conveyed reams of
wordage. Kennedy made political hay from the incident, and
Chávez again appeared as the martyr to a cause. The fast officially ended when a field altar was set up for Mass. Protestant
and Jewish speakers also gave thanks for the Great One. To
cap it off, the New Mexico sweetheart, Reies López Tijerina,
made a nonviolent speech calling for "money, guns, and
ammunition for the revolution." Had Chávez been sincere
about the initial impetus for his fast, the Tijerina speech

should have sent him back for more spiritual calories. Yet, Chávez continued to nip at his milkshakes and his grilled sandwiches. Propaganda again gave Chávez a victory among the urban chic.

The boycott of supermarkets carrying non-union grapes finally had an impact on the growers. On July 30, 1970, growers and UFWOC signed a contract. The contract, negotiated in secret between union leaders and the growers, left the worker again the displaced person in the hierarchy of production. At no time was a general collective bargaining election held prior to the signing of the contract. Workers were dismayed. They genuinely believed that the growers would not buckle under to the Chávez pressure. Yet, on the morning of July 30, the major growers of the Delano area forced compulsory unionism and a closed shop on the workers.

Chávez' contract for the workers had no opportunity for ratification by them. It made union membership a prerequisite for employment and the UFWOC could demand that a worker not in good standing be sacked. The union became the sole arbiter of the standing of a member. Here was an opportunity for Chávez and his motley crew to avenge themselves on workers who had opposed UFWOC's organizing activities. In addition, the union could demand that a worker be fired without giving cause. Workers forced into the contractual relationship found that union dues, plus back dues, plus no overtime and very little incentive pay left them with less money than before the day the contracts were signed. Probably the most malignant aspect of the contract involved the compulsion upon all workers to join the union if they wanted to work in the grape fields of Delano. Compulsory unionism, a sacrosanct principle of the Chávez coterie, became a yoke upon the workers of Delano. César Chávez, darling of the media and the liberal community, became a labor czar and attempted to impose his brand of unionism on the agricultural production of the nation.

Disposition of Hispano lands in New Mexico erupted into

a generalized cause célèbre in the mid-sixties. Integral to the
issue emerged traditional land-holding patterns of the Hispano villages, and, in addition, alleged violation of treaty
rights added to Hispano discontent. A long series of legal and
extra-legal maneuvers by government agencies and private individuals successfully removed increasing acreages of Hispano
lands from village control, and, as a result, leaders emerged to
protest the loss of traditional patrimony. Protest took violent
and non-violent forms, and the conflict developed more general social, economic, and political implications.

Legal and de facto persecution of the Spanish American
has long involved the basic rights to property and an independent means of livelihood. The concept of common village
lands that involved common pasturage and woodlots found
articulation as early as the sixteenth century and was incorporated as a part of the legal framework that governed Spain's
American empire. The reduction of these common lands
became the disputed pieces of turf of the 1960s as Hispanos
viewed their lot as an increasing rip-off of their heritage.

Guarantees of common lands granted by the Spanish
Crown and the subsequent Mexican governments of New
Mexico were incorporated into the Treaty of Guadalupe
Hidalgo of 1848. The Treaty guaranteed the civil and property
rights of Mexican citizens within the ceded territories. The key
paragraph regarding property can be found in Article VIII. It
stated:

> In the said Territories, property of every kind, now belonging to
> Mexicans and established there, shall be inviolably respected.
> The present owners, the heirs of these, and all Mexicans who may
> hereinafter acquire said property by contract shall enjoy with
> respect to it guarantees equally ample as if the same belonged to
> citizens of the United States.

These guarantees, however, were observed more in the
breach than in the practice. *Ricos* joined Anglo politicians in

the dispossession of village lands. By 1910, approximately 70 percent of Spanish and Mexican land grants, both private and communal, changed hands. Accompanying the rapid shifts of ownership came the fencing of traditionally common pastures. In northern New Mexico, in Tierra Amarilla and the Chama River area, large pastures that were once considered free range were fenced, and the Hispano herdsmen driven off.

Just prior to New Mexico's statehood (1912), sounds of alarm became apparent among the Hispanos. Department of the Interior officials, the administrators of the territories, refused to uphold the terms of the Treaty and would only recognize land patents. The courts became the final arbiters. In most instances, the Anglo litigants won the court battles.

The creation of national forests in New Mexico additionally chewed up lands owned by the Hispano villages of northern New Mexico. Between 1938 and 1965 national forests in Taos County increased in size approximately 100,000 acres or 29 percent. These lands were fenced and their use restricted, thus limiting the available lands to the Hispano herdsman. As a result, the villagers became legatees of governmental largesse, having to apply for grazing permits and restricting their herds to assigned pastures. If the cattle or sheep strayed, they were subject to impoundment by Smokey Bear and his crew. Impoundment also entailed the payment of fines or the loss of pasturing privileges on these lands as well as the loss of the impounded cattle. By 1965, the number of permits granted in the Taos National Forest diminished markedly. In 1947, there existed 350 grazing permits and free permits for milk cows, bulls, and horses. By the mid-1960's, however, these dropped to 140 and no free access for milk cows, bulls, or horses.

Conditions in northern New Mexico demanded resolution. Yet the Hispanos remained disorganized in the main, despite efforts by such groups as the *Gorras Blancas* to avenge the Hispano against the Anglo. No Hispano of sufficient

leadership ability and charismatic appeal had emerged in New
Mexico to lead the fight for the land grants. By 1960, it seemed
that such a leader might emerge in New Mexico. But he was
not a local product.

Reies López Tijerina was born in Falls City, Texas, in
1926. Very early, as a result of an extremely religious mother,
López Tijerina showed signs of a mystical bent. Visions in
childhood helped shape some of his projects in adult life. His
father was a migrant farm worker and former land owner who
suffered the indignity of being run off his land in Texas. When
Tijerina was sixteen years old, a Baptist preacher gave him a
New Testament. He became a Protestant, attended a theologi-
cal school, and became an itinerant preacher. López Tijerina
gained a reputation as a fine orator, and he wandered all over
the western United States preaching, accompanied by his wife
and six children. By 1950, he proved too unorthodox for the
church, and his credentials were revoked.

Various experiments in the founding of communal situa-
tions in Arizona and recruiting trips to New Mexico failed to
bring López Tijerina any sense of solace. Instead, violence
seemed to accompany his efforts. His incarceration and subsequent release in Arizona convinced him that he should move to
New Mexico in an attempt to rebuild his vision of a peaceful
village existence.

In New Mexico, Tijerina began to formulate a more
precise plan for action. His contacts in Chama produced sufficient evidence for him that the Hispanos were victims of governmental indifference and callousness. He decided that the
best way to fight this was through the land grants that constituted part of New Mexico's patrimony. He made contact with
the Abiquiu Corporation, a descendant of the *Gorras Blancas,*
that reveled in fence cutting and field burning.

Reies López Tijerina became the "outhouse" lawyer of the
land grant crusade. He traveled in Mexico and the Southwest,

studying the various laws that pertained to the New Mexico land grants. Increasingly he became convinced that the Hispanos were victims of Anglo rapacity. He noted that starvation conditions prevailed in some villages because the villagers no longer possessed sufficient land to earn an existence.

In 1958, Tijerina began to formulate his ideas. He approached Alfonso Sánchez, the assistant district attorney for Santa Fe County, for assistance in forming the *Alianza Federal de Mercedes* or the Federal Land Grant Alliance. Sánchez repulsed him, deploring the implied violence of the *Alianza*. From that point onward, Tijerina maintained an unabated antagonism for Sánchez. To Tijerina, Sánchez represented the worst sort of Mexican-American, the *vendido*, the *Tío Taco*.

Five years later, on February 2, 1963, the *Alianza* was formed and was incorporated in October of that year. Their headquarters at the time consisted of an abandoned warehouse in Albuquerque. Their declared intent was to "organize and acquaint the heirs of all the Spanish Land Grants covered by the Guadalupe Hidalgo treaty . . . thus providing unity of purpose and securing for the heirs of Spanish Land Grants the highest advantages as provided by the aforesaid treaty and Constitutions [of the United States and New Mexico]."

By 1966, Reies López Tijerina was ready to begin his move against the Anglo exploiters. In July, the crusade began. Five hundred *Alianza* members marched to the steps of the capitol to voice their grievances to Governor Jack Campbell. Campbell agreed to send the *Alianza* argument to the White House. Yet there was inaction in Washington.

Three months later the Echo Amphitheater in the Kit Carson National Forest was invaded by 350 *Alianza* members. These Hispanos attempted to establish their own government, and they tried two rangers for trespassing on their land. Police arrived along with FBI agents and federal marshals. A brief stand-off was followed by the disarming of *Alianza* members.

Tijerina continued to agitate for action with regard to the

land grant question. In April, 1967, the *Alianza* staged a demonstration in Albuquerque and Santa Fe. Tijerina raged from a bandstand, heaping warnings and advice on the government of New Mexico. Newly installed Governor David Cargo met with Tijerina and other *Alianza* members, proved sympathetic, but declared that he could do nothing. At the end of April, a warehouse at the Echo Amphitheater was vandalized, and fires broke out in the Kit Carson National Forest. Cargo warned Tijerina that such violence could only damage his cause.

Meanwhile, Tijerina sought allies among other Chicano leaders. He invited Rudolfo "Corky" González to come to Coyote for a meeting of the *Alianza*. He also promised González that San Joaquín would be in *Alianza* hands by June 3. In May, therefore, fires broke out throughout northern New Mexico, and the Forest Service offered a reward for the arrest of the arsonists. In March of that year the Secretary of Agriculture failed to attend a meeting sponsored by the Home Education and Livelihood Program (HELP), the Federal Economic Opportunity Project, and the Catholic Church. Instead, the assembled participants were treated to a felicitous speech by the regional forester on land use. He explained that the forest was for all to use, not merely the ranchers. More militant Hispano ranchers called the Forest Service an occupational army and wondered why a rabbit received more grass than a cow.

The meeting in March, 1967, probably precipitated the violence that occurred throughout the spring of that year. It was the way of the Abiquiu Corporation. Fences were cut. Selective cattle rustling occurred. Irrigation ditches were damaged, and arson and water tank destruction punctuated the senseless attack on Anglo ranchers. Río Arriba began to mobilize for a long range war. Governor Cargo attempted to defuse the conflict.

Meanwhile, Alfonso Sánchez became district attorney of Río Arriba. Yet despite the animosity that Tijerina felt toward him, Sánchez refused to place the blame on the *Alianza* for the vandalism and arson. Sánchez, sensitive to Tijerina's accusations of *vendido,* did not want to move precipitously against a Mexican-American. Yet the violence continued.

At the same time villagers felt increased resentment toward the San Juan-Chama Diversion Project that was to divert river waters for more efficient irrigation. This project imported labor rather than hiring from a labor force in northern New Mexico that was 80 percent unemployed. Thus, against a background of violence, unemployment, and general resentment, a rally was held at Coyote, and the *Alianza Federal de los Pueblos Libres* (Federal Alliance of Free Villages) replaced the *Alianza Federal de Mercedes.* More haystacks burned. A federal judge ordered Tijerina to submit a list of *Alianza* members, and Tijerina refused.

With the calling of the *Alianza* meeting at Coyote, tension increased. Forest Service employees sent their dependants out of the area, in case open violence dominated the scene. By this time Tijerina was accused of Communist affiliation, and New Mexico authorities girded themselves for the conflict. On the night of June 3, 1967, Sánchez issued warrants for the arrest of known *Alianza* members. Eighteen of them were arrested, but Tijerina was not among them. However, two of his brothers were caught in the dragnet. In the trunk of the car belonging to Cristóbal Tijerina supposed battle plans were found, as well as lists of the *Alianza* membership. Prominent on the list was the wife of Governor David Cargo. While officials thought they had defused the conflict, they were unprepared for the next stage.

The eighteen prisoners were interned at the Río Arriba courthouse. On June 5, four cars and a pickup truck carried twenty men and their weapons. They burst into the courthouse looking for Sánchez in order to arrest him. They failed in this, but released the prisoners, shot Patrolman Nick Sais and the jailer, and then fled, taking with them a deputy sheriff and a UPI reporter. At the same time a "picnic" of *Alianza* members was in progress. State police and New Mexico National Guardsmen converged on the Lebya farm and rounded up picnickers. Reies Tijerina was not among the group, but he finally surrendered himself.

Tijerina faced trial in November, 1967, for the amphitheater affair. A conspiracy charge was dismissed, though he was convicted of two counts of assault and sentenced to two years in prison and five years probation. He appealed his conviction and was out again on bond. His pending trial did not deter Tijerina from his activities. His increasing militancy ultimately alienated such powerful figures as Senator Joseph Montoya of New Mexico. Tijerina's polarized postures gained him admiration of the militants. When he participated in the Poor People's Campaign he emerged as an independent leader. He threatened to pull the Chicanos out of the campaign if the Black leadership did not accord them proper treatment.

In the fall of 1968, Tijerina stood trial for the courthouse affair. He was tried separately from the other defendants, and Sánchez hammered away at Tijerina with charges of assault on a jail, false imprisonment, and kidnapping. Tijerina, after much hassle, finally chose to represent himself, and ultimately the jury acquitted him. Yet, he still stood convicted of the amphitheater affair.

In 1969, Tijerina's conviction was upheld by the Tenth Circuit Court of Appeals, and his lawyer took the case to the Supreme Court. While the legal eagles argued, Tijerina opted for more direct action. On June 5, 1969, he again attempted to occupy the Coyote Campsite of the Kit Carson National Forest. On June 7, rangers arrested the occupants, Tijerina resisted arrest, and threatened a ranger with a rifle. He was charged with complicity in the destruction of government property and with assault on a federal agent. For this he received a three-year sentence.

Meanwhile, Chief Justice Warren Burger was dragged into the affair. On October 13, he refused to hear the amphitheater case, and Tijerina began serving his two sentences concurrently. For seven months he was kept in solitary confinement by prison officials who feared that he might come to harm. To the activists he became a symbol of the political prisoner. He was released in 1971.

Tijerina poses a strange phenomenon. Obviously he is in direct contrast to the more quiet Chávez, but both possess the charismatic quality so essential to the caudillo image. Tijerina is a demagogue and less a manipulator. He appeals more to gut feelings and less to machinations. Yet, the caudillo theme runs strongly through the activities of both men.

Both Chávez and Tijerina knowingly or unknowingly punctuated their efforts with violence. Both became symbols for the general Chicano movement. They became actual manifestations of pressure tactics, and the ease with which Anglo liberals could be conned.

It cannot be argued that the Hispanos of northern New Mexico were not abused. Systematic dispossession of their lands by government and private corporations in the past clearly left the Hispanos without much means of support. At the same time the violence engendered by a Tijerina increased the polarity between Hispano and Anglo and rendered the Hispano argument less viable. In contrast to the grape strike, the land grant dispute without the violent overtones clearly deserves a more judicious consideration. Unfortunately, the increased militancy of the 1960s and its concomitant Chicano chauvinism militated against the resolution of outstanding problems.

The Mexican-American and the Socio-Political Order

Advent of the new militancy of the Mexican-American has thrust the Chicano more and more into the limelight as a political force in the Southwest, Texas, and California. Suddenly a Chicano consciousness grips the region and, to a degree, the nation, for next to the Negro, the Chicano is the second largest identifiable, ethnic minority in the United States. The flood of agricultural migrants that came to the

United States during and after World War II caused a mush-
rooming of the Mexican-American population to the degree
that this ethnic group has become a "problem" for the dominant Anglo culture. Such a problem needs extirpation, and
Anglo cultural purity must be maintained. Be serious!

Urbanization has characterized the Mexican-American
who remained resident in the United States. After World War
II Mexican-Americans crowded into major cities throughout
California and the Southwest, forming enclaves of ethnic
togetherness, clinging to each other for security in an alien
land that at least covertly despised the culture they represented. In the barrios, or Mexican neighborhoods, of Los
Angeles, San Diego, Phoenix, Tucson, etc., etc., "little Mexicos" are recreated time and time again. Stores bear Mexican
names such as *La Guadalupana, Flor de la Frontera,* and
Carnicería Modelo. These are blatant testimony to the desire of
the Mexican-Americans to maintain some grip on their ethnic
roots and at the same time shield themselves from the encroachments of the Anglo world. Spanish language movie
houses also dot the barrios, and films primarily from Mexico
are shown to a Spanish-speaking clientele without the benefit
of subtitles for the occasionally curious Anglo that might
wander in on a slumming spree. While the Mexican-American
who lives in a barrio might be employed outside it, he returns
every night for cultural reenforcement. Interestingly enough,
many residents of the barrios do not have low incomes. Rather,
they feel more comfortable among people to whom Spanish is
not foreign and in whom the traditions of centuries are
ingrained.

There are, however, signs of change in the solidarity of the
barrios. More and more Mexican-Americans achieve educational successes and therefore leave the places of childhood.
The Mexican-American community, if such communal cohesiveness exists, is becoming more and more subject to deser-
tions by some of its younger members. Educational opportunities opened avenues of advancement for Mexican-Americans

that before the early 1960s did not exist. For example, federal funding of higher education allowed talented but financially-strapped Mexican-Americans to go to college and achieve a higher employment potential. This factor of social mobility, however, caused some problems for those moving into an emergent Mexican-American middle class.

Thus, a factor of social mobility exists for the Mexican-American, despite the cultural and racial prejudices that affect the great majority of them. This mobility implies a greater assimilation into the dominant Anglo culture. Middle-class Mexican-Americans soon achieve a disdain for the barrio and for any intimate association with it. What often keeps them connected with the barrio is family and extended kinships. But once out of the barrio, conscious attempts are made to drop some of the obvious Mexican trappings. The first to go is the Spanish Christian name. Carlos becomes Charles, Juan changes to John, Jaime converts to James. Of course those with names such as Jesús have a little more trouble making the change, but rest assured that their children will not be stuck with the Mexican onus.

In the alien world in which the barrio Mexican finds himself, he encounters factors that either through intent or ignorance discriminate against him. First of all, language becomes a problem. Spanish to the Anglo is foreign and a bit disreputable. To the Mexican-American seeking to break out of the barrio, speaking Spanish practically becomes anathema. For that matter, they often do not know Spanish because their parents, in a misguided attempt to force their children to be more like the Anglo, refused to speak it at home where the primary language contact would occur. In effect, social mobility, at least from the Mexican-American point of view, is facilitated by the rejection of one's original language. Implicitly, rejection of the language also means an ultimate rejection of an entire culture system, for language is the principal vehicle of culture.

As the Mexican-American moves up the social ladder, his

religious practices change appreciably. In the barrios religious holidays were observed with much the same fervor that is seen in Mexico. Processions, parties, general merrymaking characterize the celebration of a saint's day, a baptism, a confirmation, the feast of Corpus Christi, etc., etc., etc. To the middle-class Anglo and especially to the middle-class Mexican-American this is practically paganish idolatry. Why? Because in middle-class America even the Catholics act like a bunch of Calvinists. Such goings-on are unseemly. Really, isn't lighting a votive candle to a saint just a bit paganish? The poor aspiring middle-class Mexican-American has forgotten, either consciously or unconsciously, that in Mexico and in the barrio the Church is more than merely a perfunctory observance on Sundays and other holidays. It is, in fact, a corporate body acting in unison and in celebration of a particular religious event. It is a means of a community's coming together with a mutual purpose. Such communality implies more than sitting in a Church together. Implicitly, it is the laity acting together in celebration in and out of the church edifice. Therefore, the abhorrence of traditional religious celebrations by arriviste Mexican-Americans is still another negation of their primary culture.

As if kissing off Jesus and language weren't enough, the middle-class Mexican-American often becomes pushy vis-à-vis the children. The kids must excel, they must socialize with their peers, they must have material goods comparable to their peers. Moreover, traumas must not be inflicted upon them if they are to adjust adequately to society. Traditional restraints on both boys and girls are broken down, and Benjamin Spock and his permissive disciples are imposed upon the more mobile members of *la raza*.

In the barrios, however, attempts are still made to instill a sense of discipline. These attempts, of course, are often negated by pressures external to the family. The younger Mexican-

Americans want to make the leap out of the barrio and become rebellious toward the restraints imposed by parents and the barrio culture.

All of these pretensions to reach the top of the social ladder usually have minimal results. Anglo Babbitts look upon Mexican-American Babbitts as arrivistes who have nothing to recommend them except a little extra money. To many an Anglo they are still Mexicans aping the *mores* and actions of their betters. It would be preferable, reason the status-conscious Anglo Babbitts, if they would stay with their own kind and realize that money does not whiten.

This fundamentally racial attitude vis-à-vis the Mexicans has deep historical roots in the past of the United States. Throughout the nineteenth century "white" culture was destined to take over the brown skinned peoples of the hemisphere. The inferiority of those poor benighted folk was readily apparent to anyone who would open his eyes; therefore, the United States was morally bound to uplift the heathen.

Mexican-Americans, on the other hand, often view the Anglo with disdain but also with pity. Discounting the arriviste Mexicans to whom tacos and enchiladas are simply too déclassé and who view their less fortunate brethren with a certain abhorrence, Mexican-Americans feel sorry for the Anglos. They sympathize with his hectic, hurly-burly, ulcer-producing existence. They view his spiritual life as a massive vacuum that is unfulfilled because of the overweening quest for money. The poor Anglo needs to relax. This is not to say, however, that the Mexican-Americans live merely for a fulfilled spirit. Yet, they attempt to achieve a balance between the material and the spiritual that apparently has been bled out of the Anglo for centuries.

Despite all this, the diversity extant within the Mexican-American community does not make that group a cohesive

political force. The Mexican-American has failed significantly to produce a single political bloc capable of massive political action. Unlike the Negro who recently has become much
more unified, the Mexican-American's politics are often predicated upon their social-economic status rather than upon
some amorphous idea of racial or ethnic solidarity. Every political stripe is represented, ranging from screaming militants to
the more moderate LULAC.

One reason for such disparity is the Mexican-American
view that they are not, in fact, a minority group in the region
of their heaviest concentration. Thus, the disparate political
groupings do not have the militant cohesion that has been
brought to the Black civil rights struggle. While numerically a
minority throughout the nation, the Mexican-American of the
Southwest and southern California does not consider himself
as such. He has lived there for generations and has settled into
a niche, comfortable or not. His various political groupings
are characterized by infighting between groups rather than cooperation. Moreover, political leadership has been a new phenomenon in the past fifteen years, and some of the political
leaders in the Mexican-American community have not appealed to all segments of that group. As a result, money has not
been forthcoming.

This is not to say that the Mexican-Americans as a group
are impoverished and incapable of giving funds to political
groupings. Quite the contrary. Yet, the wealthy Mexican-
Americans distrust the new political leaders and view them as
ethnic troublemakers. Therefore, Mexican-Americans who
could afford the political fling refuse to contribute to ethnic
campaigns.

A telling example is the election of Congressman Henry B.
González in San Antonio in 1961. González was elected in a
special election in that year. In running, however, he demonstrated acute political acumen. González realized that a campaign could not be launched on an ethnic plank, and since

1961 he has not depended upon Mexican-American organizations for exclusive support. His appeal is sufficiently broad to bring in traditional Democratic machinery as well as the usual collection of liberal Anglos who feel that they expiate guilt by supporting a member of a minority group.

Preponderant membership by Mexican-Americans has, however, been with the Democratic party. In part, this has been the result of the Democratic bill of goods that the Republicans are the party of the rich. Vote buying through welfare programs and promises to improve the material lot of the Mexican-American have firmly tied him to the Democratic party. Nevertheless, the Mexican-American political organizations often posture as bipartisan groups, willing to deal with Mexicans of either party. In practice, however, the Mexican-American has usually gone for the Democratic candidates.

In voting for preponderantly Democratic candidates, the Mexican-American finds himself perched on the horns of a dilemma. The strongly welfare-oriented programs emanating from New Deal days provide a modicum of financial security for many Mexican-Americans. At the same time, such a dependence upon a seeming dole militates against the fiercely independent nature of most Mexican-Americans. Instances have been recorded of the indignity of accepting a handout. Of course, a preponderant number find themselves trapped into welfare assistance. Children and adults must eat, and often jobs are not available to the unskilled Mexican whose knowledge of English is, at best, limited.

During the election of 1960, the principal contenders, John F. Kennedy and Richard M. Nixon, bid for support. Mexican-Americans overwhelmingly threw their support to Kennedy. In fact, he received approximately 98 percent of the Mexican-American vote. The basic difference between the two candidates, at least as far as the Mexican-American was concerned, was not program. Both promised approximately the same thing, except that Nixon implied that he could do it at less cost. Political rhetoric is really nothing more than intellectual flatulence, anyway, but the method of delivery was important. Kennedy possessed a charisma that Nixon lacked. Despite his California origins, Nixon still smacked too much of a Protestant Middle West that generally proved inimical to the Mexican-American.

Moreover, Kennedy possessed two other qualities that assisted him in gathering the Mexican-American vote. First of all, his family came to his aid. The Kennedys as a political family have been popular and appealing. Teddy Kennedy, now Senator Kennedy, stumped throughout the Southwest and California, organizing Viva Kennedy clubs among the Mexican-Americans. There was frenzy among the Mexican-Americans for the Kennedys. Another family factor was John Kennedy's wife, Jacqueline. This aloof sophisticate was attractive, wealthy in her own right, and spoke Spanish. It was too studied, the grammar too correct, and the pronunciation resembled that of a beginning Spanish student bleating into a tape recorder. Nevertheless, the Mexican-Americans threw their support to the young, tousle-headed Senator from Massachusetts.

Secondly, the Kennedy religion, Roman Catholicism, became a decisive factor in appealing to the Mexican-American vote. Not since Al Smith in 1928, had a Catholic made a bid for the presidency, and conditions had changed since then. A wave of Mexicans crossed into the United States during and after World War II. This, plus the natural birthrate among Mexicans already resident in the United States, formed a potentially powerful voting bloc in 1960. Now a Catholic had a chance. By implication, Kennedy used his Catholicism as a means of garnering votes in the presidential contest. The Mexican-Americans responded and delivered an overwhelming vote, despite the fact that the Irish Catholicism of the Kennedys was thoroughly Puritanical and denatured. Anyway, this proves the universality of the Faith!!

The New Frontier initiated by the Kennedy Camelot failed initially in its assistance to ethnic groups. Not until after Kennedy's death did a civil rights bill pass the Congress in 1964. Yet, the Kennedy image persisted in its appeal to many Mexican-Americans. Robert Kennedy, junior senator from New York, began challenging Lyndon B. Johnson for the Presidency in 1968. Bobby, after the death of his brother, became increasingly disaffected with LBJ. Johnson's increased bellicosity in Viet Nam and the growing domestic disenchantment with the Southeast Asian imbroglio gave Kennedy an opening for a break with Lyndon.

He launched his campaign in the spring of 1968. He stumped fervently throughout California, making appeals to all disaffected groups to join the ranks against the Johnson policy. Moreover, Bobby pitched especially to the Mexican-Americans and gave particular emphasis to the agricultural workers. He became a close acquaintance of César Chávez, leader of the grape pickers' strike in Delano. Then, on June 7, the California primary was won by Kennedy. Early the next morning a crazed assassin killed the second political Kennedy. The wind was knocked out of the opposition to Johnson, who already was out of the running. Halfhearted attempts to revive the Kennedy movement died with its leader. The Democratic Convention nominated Hubert Humphrey, and the Democrats lost California in 1968.

What all this means is that the Democrats have been able to field a more charismatic group in an attempt to gather ethnic votes. Personable, attractive candidates like the Kennedys had an innate appeal to a group that based political decisions upon personalistic grounds rather than cold, hard fact. Such subjective decision-making on the part of the Mexican-American grounded itself in the political system inherited from Mexico. Caudillos, or charismatic leaders, have long characterized Mexican politics; even today, despite the depersonalization that has occurred in the Mexican body politic, political decisions still find a personalist root. Thus, the Kennedys, with their charisma and their exaggerated promises of a new mañana, capitalized upon this essential characteristic of Mexican political behavior and garnered an inordinate number of votes.

The Republicans, on the other hand, have paid little attention to this political fact. In the Southwest and California, the heavy concentration of Mexican-American votes can swing an election for one party or the other. While the Democrats have built upon what they can do for the Mexican-American, the Republicans have failed to appeal to other essential characteristics of the Mexican: a supreme conviction that he is worth something as a human being and his defense of his individuality. Republican campaigners do not make the pitch that individual endeavor, supported by extant legislation, will accomplish more than any welfare program no matter how generous.

A faint glimmer of this individualistic thrust can be seen in San Antonio, Texas, just prior to the presidential election of 1968. Three candidates held the limelight: Richard M. Nixon, the Republican also-ran who finally became president; Happy Warrior Hubert Horatio Humphrey; and George C. Wallace, the latter-day Dixiecrat threat from Alabama. All three candidates campaigned heavily in Texas, and ultimately Humphrey succeeded in gaining that state's electoral votes. But what is important is the minor boomlet among some Mexican-Americans in San Antonio for Wallace. The Viva Wallace movement in San Antonio was characterized as an attempt to put the two major parties on notice: they should not take the Mexican-American vote for granted. Mexican-Americans would vote as they damned well pleased and plethoras of promises from Nixon and Humphrey would be of no avail. For too long the major parties promised things upon which they had no intention of delivering. Thus, some Mexican-Americans, an insignificant minority admittedly, broke ranks and beat the Wallace drum. Of import here is the fact that this small group recognized in themselves that element of individualism characterizing the Mexican-American. In effect, this group told members of the Mexican-American community that they had sold out to the two major parties. While Wallace certainly had his defects, he represented a clear-cut departure from the directions of the other two parties.

In recent presidential elections, the Mexican-American vote has remained heavily Democratic. While the Kennedy phenomenon of 1960 pulled 98 percent of the vote for the Democratic party, Mexican-American support of Democrats dropped appreciably during the two elections of 1968 and 1972. In 1972, Democrat candidate George McGovern garnered approximately 85 percent of the Mexican-American vote. In 1976, President Jimmy Carter brought the percentage up to 92 percent. Carter's campaigned aimed at the Mexican-American vote through political advertisements in Spanish and capitalized on the general distrust of government held by Mexican-Americans. In light of the Watergate debacle, this basic *desconfianza* vis-á-vis the government was exacerbated, and candidate-now-President Carter successfully put more Mexican-Americans and other Spanish surname folks back into the Democratic column.

The new militant political groupings that have arisen in the 1960s and that have declared their Mexican-American militancy have, in fact, taken advantage of the charismatic leader and the appeal to an assertion of individuality. Principal among these types of leaders are César Estrada Chávez of California and Reies López Tijerina of New Mexico. César Estrada Chávez, however, can be seen more as a labor leader, willing to wield power, but along less political lines. His principal stance in the grape strike in California was primarily economic rather than directly political.

Reies López Tijerina, however, epitomizes the charismatic political leader of the new Mexican-American militancy. His *Alianza Federal de los Pueblos Libres* bases itself upon the guarantees given to Mexican citizens in New Mexico at the time of the Treaty of Guadalupe Hidalgo. In that document, the United States promises not to violate personal, private, and cultural rights of Mexicans in the new territory. However, encroachments upon Mexican lands by private landholders, by the Forest Service, and by State Government whittled away the lands held by New Mexicans prior to 1848.

López Tijerina's politics are in many ways representative of the New Militancy. He has, however, given it an international flavor. As early as 1962, López Tijerina sought to drag Mexico into the land dispute. He argued that both signatories to the Treaty of Guadalupe Hidalgo were bound to respect the cultural rights of each other's citizens. In effect, Mexico should bring diplomatic pressure to bear upon the United States government to assure that the Hispanos of New Mexico will have their lands restored and their culture vindicated. Thus, Tijerina chose to link property rights with the rights of an indigenous culture to maintain itself. Tijerina chose ethnic politics. The Governor of New Mexico, David Cargo, had been sympathetic to the plight of the Hispanos but equivocated in giving full support to the movement for a restoration of lands. Politics being what it is, the Governor was forced to count heads to determine the political feasibility of such a maneuver. Thus, Cargo, who in 1964 seemed reasonable and sympathetic to the Hispanos, began to hedge his political bets.

In 1968, López Tijerina's political movement broadened. Martin Luther King, the assassinated Civil Rights leader, chose Tijerina as his personal choice to coordinate the Poor People's March in New Mexico. While Tijerina did not personally make the trip to Washington, the March thrust the *Alianza Federal* into a broadened political arena. It linked the Hispano demands with those of deposed Negroes in the South. But there were problems with this close union. Hispano members objected to the domination of policy making by members of the Southern Christian Leadership Conference. This, in turn, underscored some of the essential problems extant in inter-ethnic politics.

Essentially, a great deal of tension exists between the Negroes and the Mexican-Americans. Even the superficial co-operation between the Hispanos and the late Martin Luther King showed that ultimately the better organized Blacks dominated the Poor People's Campaign. In larger urban concentrations such as Los Angeles, Tucson, and Phoenix, not to mention the large Texas cities, Negro-Mexican-American co-operation rarely exists. Both groups suffer the ignominious position of being at the bottom of the social heap and both are struggling to get out of it. They compete with each other, and as a result also bicker and fight at cross-purposes. Each group, it should be noted, has its own peculiarities that will not necessarily be reconciled, even for a short period of time, in order to achieve a political objective.

Probably the most trenchant argument in support of Tijerina's demands that the Hispano culture be respected can be seen in the conflict between Mexican-Americans and Anglos in the public schools in the Southwest and California. The tendency in public schools has been to prohibit the speaking of Spanish either in the classroom or on the school premises. This trend blatantly indicates the Anglo belief in the superiority of its culture to that of the Mexican-American. In New Mexico, where Spanish is considered an official language, the process of acculturation for the Hispanos went rather smoothly before World War II. After 1940, as more and more Mexicans from Mexico made their way to the United States, either legally or illegally, bilingualism lost ground. After the war, the desire for more laborers from Mexico kept the wave coming from south of the Rio Grande, and the schools were not equipped to handle children who spoke Spanish exclusively.

Throughout the Southwest and California, therefore, Spanish became a big No, No in the public schools. Children were disciplined severely for communicating with each other in the only language they understood. The net effect of such an arbitrary prohibition of Spanish has been a reduction in the learning potential of Spanish-speaking students. Students whose primary language is Spanish do not perform well on general intelligence tests or aptitude surveys. The simple fact is that they do not comprehend the questions because the teachers have not taught them English. Rather, they have prohibited the use of Spanish without using it as a viable springboard for teaching English.

In Texas, for example, the prevalent view is that children should know how to speak English almost right from the womb. What the hell, they're Americans, aren't they? Yet the reality, so aptly documented by George I. Sánchez of the University of Texas, clearly indicates the exact opposite. Even the Texas Education Agency admitted that many Spanish-speaking children had to spend two years in the first grade because they knew only Spanish. The net effect is frustration, a high dropout rate, joblessness, and a perpetuation of prejudice on both sides.

The dropout hates the system that caused him educational failure. He cannot get a job because he lacks a high school diploma. He lacks the diploma because he could not learn enough English to make the grade. He did not learn English because he was never properly instructed in the language. At the same time, the teachers and members of a dominant Anglo society continue to view the high dropout rate among Mexican-Americans as clear evidence that those poor dumb Mexicans really can't learn a hell of a lot anyway. They were incapable of making it in the dominant educational system so they shouldn't be given too much consideration.

Sánchez recommends a bilingual approach to instruction of the Mexican-American child, Spanish-speaking teachers should be employed to instruct children whose native language is Spanish. Therefore, English would be taught as a second language, and gradually the child would learn enough English to be instructed in that language. The reality is that these children will live in an English dominated culture and should, therefore, have a grasp of that language. Yet, there is nothing inferior about Spanish. Children educated in a bilingual system would have the advantages of bilingualism without the linguistic frustrations that to the present time have caused high dropout rates among Mexican-American children.

But there exists a factor that militates against bilingual education: namely, the resistance for biculturalism in the dominant Anglo schools of education. These academic refuse heaps instead burden their students with countless courses in methodology and educational "theory" instead of an emphasis on a good working grasp of subject matter. Of course, one could hire Mexican-Americans to teach in Spanish but the problem remains of assuring quality education. It becomes incumbent, therefore, upon the educational systems to assure an adequate supply of bilingual instructors even if it means a revamping of education schools and teacher curricula. This latter suggestion is probably a pipe dream. Nothing suffers more from inertia and status anxiety than an Educationist. However, I digress again.

The most vicious cycle that entraps the lower class Mexican-American is welfare. Meddlesome social workers, an abundance of forms, and a general mood of condescension toward the truly down-and-out make the reception of welfare assistance odious. The present welfare system, despite its good intentions, has successfully robbed the Mexican-American of his dignity and of his incentive to provide for himself. Instead, a vicious pattern is established that perpetuates welfare dependence for generations. In Santa Barbara, California, for example, there are instances of families who have been on welfare for three generations and probably will continue into a fourth generation.

In recent decades there have been attempts by Mexican-Americans themselves to break the welfare cycle and regain human dignity. In New Mexico in the mid 1960's, for example, the creation of HELP, with assistance from the New Mexico Council of Churches, the Roman Catholic Archdiocese of Santa Fe, the Ford Foundation, and the Office of Economic Opportunity of the Department of Health, Education, and Welfare, looks to give the Hispano villages of northern New Mexico a new lease on life. It hopes to develop in them a sense of community through the instigation of native industry. It aims, for example, at a tanning industry based upon the hides produced in that part of the state and up to now shipped out for tanning. Fundamentally, it is a very conservative reform program predicated upon the idea that local units such as the Hispano villages can best determine their economic patterns.

Yet the program suffers a bad press. In New Mexico, the dominant Anglos view it as suspicious at best and probably subversive. The John Birch Society publication, *American Opinion*, dubbed it as a Commie plot to wrench the Southwest from the United States. This sort of decentralized control is the essence of conservative ideas, but apparently the Birchers would like to keep decentralization for the Anglo and to hell with the Hispano. This is not to deny, however, that the possibility exists for revolutionary ferment. It is incumbent upon the village reformers to make sure that their cooperatives are not subverted by external forces bent upon the destruction of society.

In both rural and urban concentrations of Mexican-Americans, attempts are made to assure proper welfare treatment for recipients and eventual self-help and removal from the welfare rolls. In this the Office of Economic Opportunity has attempted to assist the Mexican-American through providing legal counsel. In one case, for example, a migrant farm family felt that the public school discriminated against their daughter because they wanted to place her in a special education class for retarded children. She had been administered a standard intelligence test and found to be barely trainable. The parents protested, the OEO legal eagles pressured the school system, and the child was retested in Spanish and found to be within a normal range. Unconsciously, a discriminatory act had been perpetrated because the child knew no English, and as a result the dominant culture dictated that she was lacking in gray matter.

In the more general area, the Civil Rights Acts of 1964 and 1968, buttressed by the OEO legal defense people, have cleared a juridic path for advancement by the Mexican-American. In a sense, it is like a football game. The ball is back to the Mexican-American who wishes to advance. He must exhaust available avenues for advancement now that the law clearly guarantees him certain rights against discrimination in jobs and opportunities.

Yet, the problem of condescension persists. It spreads throughout the Anglo culture in the United States. In part, the phenomenon can be traced to its historic roots and the Anglo aversion to things foreign. A sort of nativism makes it difficult for the Mexican-American to be fully accepted as a bicultural being. Instead he is viewed as different and somewhat frightening. Good Lord, he might not speak English!!

Two personal examples best illustrate this point. A few years ago, in a small college community in northern New York my wife and I attended a party given by the local jet set. In the course of conversation my wife, who is dark haired and brown eyed, was told by one of the ladies at this gathering that she spoke excellent English. My very proper wife then told her that she too spoke excellent English and further informed the condescending WASP that she had been speaking English all of her life. The point is that it was assumed that my wife was Mexican because she looks Mexican. Her royal Stuart ancestors and Daughters of the American Revolution antecedents are probably spinning like dervishes in their respective graves.

Another incident, much more recent and more telling, occurred when we adopted two Mexican children to fill out our family to four. In the summer of 1970, we adopted a two-month-old boy. We were told that he was difficult to place because he was Mexican. In March, 1971, we added a four-month-old Mexican girl who was considered utterly unadoptable because she too had the onus of being Mexican. In fact, the social worker who placed her with us stated that it was difficult to place such children with "white" families. There was no malice intended in the statement, but it certainly is indicative of a nativist ignorance that even afflicts ostensibly educated people.

In Montana, a state suffering from low budgets, child welfare services is a catch-as-catch-can operation. The social worker has total power in deciding where the children are placed. In the instance of our second adopted child, we were approached by the Welfare Department wondering if we would like to reapply because the child was already born. We vacillated. Two babies under one year of age can be a handful. But we did reapply, and it took two months to get the child home. The welfare worker sat on the papers rather than process them quickly. What is more important, however, is the power given to an inexperienced and unfortunately ignorant girl in determining the fate of a child. It was tacitly assumed that neither of our adopted children could be placed because of their Mexican origins, unless they came to a family that might also suffer the Mexican taint. I should not, however, be too bitter. We have the kids. Yet, it is indicative of the condition of a society that refuses to recognize worth in something that is different from its mainstream.

Generally, the Mexican-American is caught between a maintenance of cultural purity and adaptation to the dominant social patterns. He has been a political pawn and is beginning to react against this. As he moves up a social scale, the Mexican-American, of necessity, must cast aside the more obvious trappings of his mother culture. But down deep in his being, the Mexican-American who has moved up the social ladder in terms of position and education feels the call of *la raza*. He cannot reject totally his mixed Mexican origins. Rather, he makes outward adaptations for the sake of keeping the Anglo happy and for his own advancement.

The idea that the United States is a melting pot that accepts other cultures with open arms is pure nonsense. The discrimination against the Irish, the Poles, the Italians, and the Mexicans is clear indication that this pluralism is predicated upon the idea that these groups *must* adapt to the dominant Anglos' social patterns if they are to be accepted. Members of these groups that have adapted are necessarily schizophrenic in a cultural sense. Outwardly they play the Anglo game while inwardly the Mexican-American, for example, still wants to maintain his Mexican origins within a pluralistic society.

The Mexican-American too must come to grips with his place in a fluid society. Ethnic solidarity probably is most unworkable, for too many external pressures will rupture that sense of solidarity. Moreover, the Mexican-American needs to look at his own mixed origins. He is both Indian and Spanish, and the myth of *la raza de bronce,* or the bronze race, is just pure bunk. The Mexican or the Mexican-American is what José Vasconcelos called the *raza cósmica,* or the cosmic race: a hybrid taking the best from both Indian and Spanish cultures to produce a third stock better than the other two.

What this university needs is a 'wasp studies' department!

Jozeph 75

8

Academia and Riots

Paralleling developments in the grapefields of Delano and the mountain villages of northern New Mexico emerged a greater attempt at a definition of what it was to be a Mexican-American. In the late 1960's Chicano studies programs burgeoned in the Southwest, Texas, and California, attempting to give a sense of identity to Chicanos and their demands for social, political, and economic equality. In addition, the vast majority of Mexican-Americans were urban dwellers, residing in barrios or in more affluent nieghborhoods depending upon their economic status. Chicano militants sought to organize them into more cohesive units. The degree of organization and

135

its effectiveness still remains to be measured, but militancy can be made to seem more representative merely by the extra noise and chaos that it produces.

One of the unfortunate spin-offs of attempts to synthesize the Chicano "culture" could be seen in the increasing unrest in the barrios and in the sheer exploitation by Chicano leaders and national politicians of the very real grievances of the Mexican-Americans. False promises and false hopes have agitated segments of Mexican-American communities and have caused unfortunate backlashes, thus retarding the progress of these people. To a large degree the trend toward integral Chicano studies must share the blame for the unrest of the latter 1960's, for academicians—often a befuddled group—became champions of ethnic and minority studies, including women's studies. Chicano studies, therefore, need analysis first before the violence in the barrios of the late 1960's and early 1970's can be understood.

Viva México! Hijos de la chingada! In the language of the guttersnipe of East Los Angeles, of the WASP (White, Anglo-Saxon, Protestant) who has an infatuation for things Mexican, of the professional do-gooder who becomes horrified by the plight of our little brown brothers of Mexican extraction—this ejaculation means "Long live Mexico! Sons of bitches!" Unfortunately, such a mundane rendition, for a term that is fraught with nuance and connotation does an injustice to the Mexican-American and to his Mexican heritage. According to Octavio Paz, *la chingada* is the submissive person, usually denoted as a female, in a relationship, one who is forcibly violated either sexually or emotionally. In his *Labyrinth of Solitude* Paz poignantly describes the inner conflict of the Mexican. His country has been raped by foreigners—first Spaniards, then gringos, then French, and then a potpourri of foreign entrepreneurs during the protracted Díaz dictatorship. In the Mexican War, Mexico underwent a blow to its essential

masculine conception of itself when the country was castrated
through the loss of nearly half of its territory to the United
States. In short, the mestizo—the product of the violent conquest of the Indian by the Spaniard—hangs suspended in a
labyrinth of solitude, unsure of his origins and of his loyalties.
He is a historical orphan, hating his white father but at the
same time denigrating his Indian mother for the lowness of her
station. Often, he is rejected by both. Thus the Mexican, already unsure of his place and his identity, comes to the United
States, suffers still more rejection, and plunges into abysmal
depressions that manifest themselves in violent actions and
exaggerations of things indigenously Mexican.

Octavio Paz produced a magnificent work of defining the
essential character of the Mexican as he sees it. His work is one
of synthesis, based upon wide reading and a fundamental
understanding of his people. For the historian of Mexico in the
United States, Paz becomes a basic work. But, the *Labyrinth of
Solitude* fails to analyze in depth what happens to the Mexican
who, for one reason or another, is transplanted in *gringolan-
dia.* Paz' rendition is too superficial, for Paz overgeneralizes
about United States culture and attempts to create too much of
a gringo stereotype.

At this juncture the American social historian should step
in and analyze what has happened to the Mexican-American.
Yet, here is where the latest fad toward ethnic history falls short
of its mark. Chicano studies, or Mexican-American studies,
demand that the Mexican-American be treated as a homogeneous unit, leaving out of consideration the great variety of
cultures that comprise Mexico and the different regional units
whose essential élan militates against a Mexican homogeneity.

In part, the impulse toward a homogeneous treatment of
the Mexican-American comes from a sympathy, at times mis-
placed, for the grape pickers' strike occurring in central
California. The bulk of the grape pickers are Mexican-
Americans or recent immigrants from Mexico. The movement

initiated by Estrada Chávez and espoused by Reies Tijerina of New Mexico extends beyond a simple economic confrontation between labor and management. *La causa,* or the cause, embodies the ideals of a Mexican homogeneity that, except for mythological purposes, is nonexistent. It is assumed that all Mexican-Americans are poor, migrant laborers; it is assumed that all Mexican-Americans are of predominantly Indian stock and wish to emphasize it; it is assumed that all Mexican-Americans immediately sympathize with the heroes of the 1910 Revolution. It is moreover assumed that any Mexican-American who does not hold these views is a *Tío Taco* and has sold out to the oppressive, racist Anglos.

Unfortunately, the hallowed halls of Academe have fallen prey to the Mexican-American mythology. In California, the United Mexican-American Students or UMAS demand courses in Mexican-American history taught by professors of their choice. Professional Mexicans—those individuals who are Mexican-American by birth and mythmakers by choice—beat the drums for a greater emphasis on Mexican-American studies. To what purpose? In all probability, they attempt to exalt their own egos and to yield to the pressure for generalization and simplification engendered by the vast proliferation of knowledge. Perhaps even worse than the professional Mexican is the Anglo who has developed a fascination for Mexico and for all things Mexican. His Goody-Two-Shoes heart exudes the milk of human kindness and, in all sincerity, he deeply sympathizes with that symbol of the oppressed Mexican-American: the grape picker. This is the individual who would forcibly clean up the dens of iniquity south of the border in order to make the Mexicans behave in righteous ways and lead decent, United States type lives. Yet, this is the same ignoramus who thoroughly enjoys the titillation of a bestiality act in the Tijuana bars.

Serious monographic studies need to be done on the impact of the Mexican-American in the United States. One such work, Cecil Robinson's *With the Ears of Strangers: The*

Mexican in American Literature traces the image of the Mexican in American belles lettres from the savage, swarthy, sneaky, yet inferior Catholic through the romanticized non-sense of Helen Hunt Jackson's *Ramona* to John Steinbeck's sordid *Tortilla Flat*. Robinson's contention is that the South-west and northern Mexico comprise a culture region un-hampered by political boundaries. He argues most persua-sively that an essential interaction has occurred that has produced a culture unique to both the United States and Mexico. In this respect, he operates on a fallacious assump-tion: that the culture of northern Mexico is a deviate from a cultural mainstream south of Sonora, Chihuahua, Coahuila, and Nuevo Leon. Again, what needs greater stress is the cul-tural composition and uniqueness of Mexico's many regions.

Another recent work, quite sympathetic to the Mexican-American but unmarred by the simplistic gibberish of the Chicano and Brown Beret types, is Julián Samora's *La Raza: The Forgotten Americans*. In this work, historians, demog-raphers, educators, political scientists, and sociologists have collaborated in producing a highly important work. Analyses are made of current Mexican-American problems, but even George I. Sánchez, a leading historian of Mexican education, operates in the vacuum of the present without placing the topic in historical perspective. Thus, we are left with the Mexican-American as of 1966, but how did he get there in the first place?

Before any sort of objective appreciation of the Mexican-American can be reached, it is important to sweep away the simplistic assumptions for Mexican-American studies under which UMAS, the Brown Beret *fascisti*, and their Anglo soul brothers operate. First of all, many Mexican-Americans find it difficult to identify with the grape pickers and with immi-grant agricultural laborers. They are professional people, industrial workers, primarily urban dwellers who have severed the ties with the barrios of Los Angeles, Tucson, or El Paso. As Zamora and his colleagues show, these individuals have not negated their *mexicanidad* but have adapted to the dominant culture. They are organized into such groups as the *Unión Cívica Mexicana* which strives to keep alive the Mexican heritage without becoming fetishistic about the Virgin of Guadalupe, Miguel Hidalgo, Benito Juárez, or the pantheon of Mexican demigods who led *La Revolución* of 1910. Their social and economic aspirations are conditioned by the criteria established within the general culture rather than some far-fetched, unreachable ideal that, because of its inaccessibility, will cause frustration and bitterness.

While it is true that the Mexican-American emerges from the indigenous stock of Mexico, it is likewise untrue that all have become Indianists, or *indigenistas*. This phenomenon had its greatest impact upon Mexico in the 1920's and has persisted to this day in varying degrees of virulence. It is a total rejection of all elements in the Mexican culture that are of Spanish origin. Some extremists in Mexico, for example, go to the extent of advocating a return to Nahuatl as the Mexican lingua franca and a regression back to the ceremonial blood-letting of the Aztec priests. Discovery of the bones of Hernán Cortés in 1946 precipitated a new upsurge of militant *indigenismo* in Mexico. Fiery, militant, Dr. Eulalia Guzmán led the charge to find the bones of Cuauhtémoc, the last Aztec Emperor. With a preconceived notion in mind, the indefatigable Dr. Guzmán began digging around southern Mexico to find the hallowed relics. Finally, a mass of bones were discovered which, to nobody's astonishment, were declared to be the sacred remains. The documentation, as Lesley Bird Simpson points out in his *Many Mexicos*, was patently absurd. The bones consisted of a conglomeration from many skeletons, and in which the cranium was female. No matter!! Those were the sacred bones, and all good Mexicans had to believe in their veracity despite the definitive evidence to the contrary. A "Cuauhtémoc Week" was declared and demonstrations were held in front of the redoubtable Indian's monument on the

Paseo de la Reforma. Lesley Bird Simpson states: "Cuauhtémoc, who was certainly a stout fellow, but who was bitterly
hated by most Mexicans as the leader of the hated Aztecs, has
thus become the symbol of democratic resistance to the op-
pressor, and a pair of grim soldiers with loaded rifles guard his
grave against desecration."

To many Americans, this sort of argumentation is fundamentally pedantic nonsense. Mexico, and the Mexican-
Americans, are a blending of Spanish and Indian that has produced a mestizo. José Vasconcelos, Mexico's brilliant
philosopher and outstanding Minister of Education under
Alvaro Obregón in the early 1920's, coined the term *la raza
cósmica*. This amalgamation of indigenous and European
stock is what has given, he argues, the fortitude, will, and en-
durance to the Mexicans. The mestizo culture of Mexico and
Latin America, argued Vasconcelos, would prove more durable
than the indigenous or European stocks from which it
emerged. Moreover, the Mexican-Americans who, for example,
are members of the *Unión Cívica* feel that their first loyalty is
to the country of which they are citizens and in which they
reside. Writes one *Unión Cívica* member in Santa Barbara,
California:

> As an American of Mexican ancestory, I take exception to
> this Chicano label which is now being brainwashed by the Brown
> Berets into the minds of our younger generation. It is bad enough
> to have allowed our ethnic element to be branded Mexican-
> American when we know our loyalty as Americans comes first.

Among the heroes of the Mexican Revolution one of the
most revered is Emiliano Zapata, the land reforming bandit of
Morelos. Reies Tijerina and Estrada Chávez often receive
billing as latter day *zapatistas* carrying forth Don Emiliano's
banner of supremacy of the downtrodden to the oppressed
Mexican-American. Again, the idea that Mexican-Americans
uniformly revere Zapata, Madero, Carranza, Cárdenas et al. is

patently ridiculous. Between 1910 and 1920, the ranks of Mexicans filled in Los Angeles and the Southwest as a result of the depredations visited upon old families by the altruistic revolutionaries. Some Mexican-Americans bear deep grudges against those bandits who deprived them of their fortunes in their ancestral homeland. Therefore, to assume that the Mexican-American will automatically like Zapata merely because he is a latter-day hero is to assume that Hubert Humphrey believed in self-flagellation and voted for Richard Nixon in 1968.

The social historian faces a momentous task. To begin with, the propaganda of UMAS and the Brown Berets who espouse *la causa* must be viewed for what it is: an attempt to move through demagoguery and visceral reactions. Moreover, a new approach to American history, defined in its broadest terms, must be considered.

No longer can we operate in a vacuum. Comparative history, of necessity, dictates a competence in more than one field. Therefore, to study the Mexican-American, the historian must have a broad understanding of the multifaceted roots from which this important ethnic group emerged. Moreover, the historian needs to know the American culture equally well, for without such knowledge of both cultures he cannot appreciate nor analyze the impact of one upon members of the other. How, for example, did Mexican residents contribute to the independence of Texas in 1836? Did these same people or their descendants play a significant role in the Mexican War of 1846-1848? What adaptations have been made by Mexican-Americans in the United States? How have social, economic, political and religious practices been altered by the predominant Anglo environment? In what way has the Mexican-American proved a viable part of the United States economy and society? Taking into consideration the regional diversities of Mexico, what differences of adaptability have occurred in the United States as a result of Mexican regional uniqueness?

Has the concept of the *patria chica* dissipated in Mexican-American communities?

Separate Chicano studies programs fail to take up valid historical questions. Instead, they are dedicated to the proposition that a rip-off has been perpetrated against all Mexican-Americans and that today's Anglos should, in some way, atone for the sins of the past. Some institutions in California, for example, have burgeoning academic empires called Chicano Studies Departments or Programs. These ivory tower entities possess faculties ranging from two to three to fifteen and twenty, depending upon the degree of guilt felt by Anglo administrators and by the amount of pressure brought to bear upon these same administrators by militant Chicanos.

These programs, instead of encouraging the dispassionate study of the Mexican-American, often serve as focal points of militant action sanctioned by administrators and legislators who appropriate the money. Additionally, these ethnic programs attempt to perpetuate themselves through the creation of similar programs not yet blessed by ethnicity. This action serves as a means of creating jobs for graduates—both undergraduate and graduate—who probably would not get the jobs in legitimate academic departments. Of course in these days of economic stringency, programs are often frozen in place, graduates of such programs are often frustrated in their job searches, and they add ultimately to the general frustration in the larger community.

Even in the areas where no significant Chicano population exists, attempts have been made to introduce a full blown Chicano studies program. As early as 1970, tentative approaches were made about a Chicano studies program at the University of Montana. Luckily the attempt was squashed. That particular institution has enough trouble with other ethnic and minority programs without getting into yet another one. In 1973, I was approached by some Chicano graduate students while attending a meeting in Los Angeles. They were interested in finding out about jobs for Chicanos at the University of Montana. I was interested in determining what kind of jobs. Did they want to place Chicano microbiologists, political scientists, historians, sociologists, forestry experts, range management specialists, etc., etc.? No *mano* ("brother" or "pal"), they wanted Chicano studies! If it weren't so damned tragic, it would be laughable. Maybe it's better to laugh than to cry. The frustration, therefore, among the Chicanos who study monolithic Chicano studies increases in its impact.

The Chicano mania spread from university to barrio. Alternative education programs, often staffed by untrained and incompetent teachers, preached a gospel of separatism and Chicano nationalism. Because of the emphasis on the revolutionary and monolithic character of Chicano culture, the alternative schools preached a doctrine of revolt against the Establishment and separatism. Attempts were made, therefore, to create prepubescent malcontents who spoke neither competent English nor Spanish, and were devoid of critical faculties as a result of the chauvinistic brainwashing of such nihilistic outfits.

The accumulated impotence of Chicano studies, alternative schools, and the general militancy of college and university campuses made itself felt on August 29, 1970, the date of the Chicano National Moratorium on Viet Nam. *The result of the Moratorium was a full-scale riot in Los Angeles, the death of a respected Chicano journalist, and increasing distrust between Anglo and Chicano in the Los Angeles area.

In all probability the hassle began when Rosalío Muñoz, student body president at the University of California, Los Angeles, in 1968-1969, received his draft notice. He refused induction, and took his protest to the Chicano community in Los Angeles. Muñoz wanted to build up resistance to the Viet

---

*Much of this section is based on Patty Newman, *Do It Up Brown* (San Diego: View Point Books, 1971).

Nam war in a large way. Muñoz and people of his ilk accused the United States of planned genocide against the Chicanos, for this group constituted a greater percentage of the Armed Services than they did the general population. Therefore, more Chicanos were wounded or killed in Viet Nam proportionally than any other ethnic or racial grouping. Muñoz et al. argue that Chicanos are lured into Armed Forces in order to commit them to military activity and thereby wipe them out.

With the receipt of his draft notice, Muñoz began forming the National Chicano Moratorium Committee. Preliminary demonstrations were held throughout 1969 and early 1970, warming up for the big do in East Los Angeles. The date for the Los Angeles affair was set, Muñoz announced that nearly 100,000 Chicanos would participate in the Moratorium, and he was supported by Corky González' Chicano Youth Liberation Conference in Denver. González' crew at this time worked out the details of the *Plan de Aztlán* and formally initiated the *Raza Unida* Party as an independent political party of Chicanos.

Preparations for the National Chicano Moratorium progressed. Equipment for the rally was secured from different groups of radical persuasion in the southern California area. Speakers were lined up for the big event, among them César Chávez, and representatives of different militant Chicano groups. In fact, much of the support for the Moratorium came from outside the barrio of East Los Angeles.

As the militant troops gathered for the Moratorium, tension began to grow. As August 29 began, while the atmosphere was tense, the Moratorium parade began rather peacefully. Yet, by nightfall, three people would be killed, sixty would be injured, including twenty-eight deputy sheriffs, and over two million dollars worth of property would suffer destruction. In addition, 185 people would be arrested by those sheriff's deputies still unhurt by rioters.

As the paraders made their way toward Laguna Park, not too much seemed out of place. A few minor disturbances broke out during the parade, but in these days a minor disturbance can seem like a peaceful demonstration in relative terms. Then an incident occurred. At 1:30 in the afternoon, a liquor store not far from Laguna Park was pilfered, and the Sheriff's Department dispatched assistance to remove the approximately 300 persons who helped themselves to gallons of free booze. Rocks and bottles began to fly, backup squads were called by officers on the scene, and this subsequently inflamed the already worked up mob. Rioters fled into Laguna Park, heaving various missiles at the police. By 3:10 P.M., the assembly in Laguna Park lost its peaceful nature, became branded as an unlawful assembly, and participants were ordered to disperse. Police proceeded to move into the park with tear gas at the ready.

The riot increased in its intensity and spilled out of the park down Whittier Boulevard. Looting or the Liberation of Goods became commonplace. Sheriff's deputies ignored most looting in an attempt to quell the more violent manifestations of peaceful protest. Shots were fired; police officers were forced to use guns; the riot continued.

Late in the afternoon, around five o'clock, Rubén Salazar, a columnist for the *Los Angeles Times* and news director of the television station KMEX, wandered into the Silver Dollar Bar with some friends. The Silver Dollar Bar, while quiet inside, was surrounded by fires and unbridled brigandage. Firemen worked to stop the blaze. According to one report, sheriff's deputies ordered everyone out of the Silver Dollar three times and there was no response from inside the bar. As a result, a sheriff's deputy fired three tear gas projectiles into the bar in order to clear it out. One of these, a Flite Rite projectile, struck Rubén Salazar on the temple and killed him. A great deal of controversy arose over the death of Salazar, the use of that particular type of tear gas projectile, and the "overreaction" of police units.

Meanwhile, Corky González and some of his stalwarts tangled with sheriffs when their flatbed truck was stopped for a traffic violation and three weapons were found on board. In addition, $370 was found among the truck occupants. González called the arrests a form of police harassment of Chicanos. Arrests were made, some of those arrested chose to remain in jail while others went out on bail. Among those who elected for the Los Angeles jail was Corky González. Militants felt that the presence of Gonzalez gave some symbolic clout to the protest. However, on August 30, González was out on bail.

The next day, relative calm characterized East Los Angeles. Yet, in other sections of Los Angeles County some rioting erupted. Barrio activists met to make the death of Rubén Salazar a key issue in their attempt to underscore the nature of police brutality vis-à-vis Chicanos. Establishment and radical press in Los Angeles published plethoras of opinions about the riots and the death of Salazar. Even Mexico City newspapers jumped into the act, reflecting the diversity of opinions about the riots. Opinions ranged from murder to justifiable police action. No one seemed particularly neutral about the Salazar death and the role of the Los Angeles County Sheriff's Department. Oscar Acosta, militant Chicano attorney, argued that sheriff's deputies knew that Salazar was in the Silver Dollar and purposely killed him as a means of quelling an effective Mexican-American voice. To Acosta, this was political assassination perpetrated by the praetorians of the state. Militant rags took up the theme of a conspiracy to kill Salazar. What began as an investigation into the tragic death of a respected citizen gradually grew onto a massive propaganda effort by militant Chicanos to neutralize the inquest. What they hoped to achieve, in effect, was a trial of the Establishment through the media.

The inquest into the death of Rubén Salazar began on September 10, 1970, and lasted for sixteen days. In tangible results,. the inquest produced 2025 pages of testimony taken from sixty-one witnesses and 204 exhibits. Nothing was settled. Days and days of conflicting testimony characterized the proceedings and Chicano militants played to the cameras in an attempt to advance their point of view. Conflicting photographs, supplied by the Sheriff's Department and by militant Chicanos, further confused the problem that faced the coroner's jury.

Oscar Acosta, acting for a Blue Ribbon Committee to monitor the inquest, played buffoon during the proceedings. He led several dramatic walkouts from the hearing room. A circus atmosphere, though certainly not an entertaining one, pervaded the hearing. Emotional outbursts by militant Chicanos continually drummed home the message that the damned pigs had perpetrated political assassination against a Chicano. Acosta also attempted to make hay by interrupting the proceedings. As a spectator he had no right to participate in the hearing, yet he raised objections to lines of questioning. At one point he so irritated the hearing officer that he was forcibly removed from the hearing room. Acosta was removed, and this incident provided yet another example of ruthless police brutality for the propagandists.

Finally, the hearing reached its conclusion. Of the seven members on the coroner's jury four voted that the death was "at hands of another," and three opted for accidental death. A clamor arose for the arrest and prosecution of Deputy Thomas Wilson, the hapless person who fired the Flite Rite into the Silver Dollar Bar. Los Angeles County Attorney Evelle J. Younger, however, concluded that if any negligence was present in the incident, it was of such a minor nature that no criminal charge was justified against Wilson. Younger, a candidate for state attorney general, was accused by militants of playing to the law and order theme in order to achieve his later election. While political consideration probably played a part, to accuse Younger in such a simplistic way probably speaks more for the intellect of the accusers than for the nefariousness of the accused.

After the Chicano Moratorium riot of August 29, two other demonstrations took place that involved the police against the demonstrators. One occurred on September 16, 1970, during the celebration of Mexican Independence. Sentiments still were fevered as a result of the Moratorium fiasco, and soon militant Chicanos squared off with the police. Rock-throwing teenagers set off the police action. Police moved in, demonstrators scattered, heads were cracked. Press and television coverage condemned the marchers. Things in East Los Angeles continued to look grim.

The other incident occurred on January 9, 1971, a march organized by the Chicano Moratorium Committee convened at the Hollenbeck Police Station. Approximately 1,000 marchers then strode from Hollenbeck to Parker Center—the Los Angeles Police Headquarters—and began to picket the area. The picketers were ordered to disperse. Riots and vandalism again characterized the confusion. The police again moved quickly against the rioters and again received the opprobrium of police brutality. On the heels of this activity, a three-day march from the four largest barrios in Los Angeles terminated in a rally at Belvedere Park in East Los Angeles on January 31. Sheriff and police officers were at the ready for any expected violence. When the crowd dispersed, they marched by a police station and began taunting the policemen on duty. Soon the chants erupted into a riot. Again police and sheriff's units moved quickly: tear gas flew, some shots were fired by both sides, and the riot was finally controlled. Yet, the propagandists had more material for the mimeograph machines.

Local grievances within the barrios accounted for the riots of 1970 and 1971. Frustration of barrio existence built up to such a degree that they served as a fertile ground from which agitators could raise quite a crop. Organizers, among them the Brown Berets, the Mexican-American Political Association (MAPA), the Mexican-American Youth Organization (MAYO), the Crusade for Justice, to name a few, saw in the Los Angeles barrios an opportunity to force a confrontation with the Establishment. In this they proved successful. At the same time they used individuals recruited from Chicano studies programs as a means of lending a degree of respectability to their activities.

In many respects the Chicano studies programs must bear some of the blame for the violence that has marred Anglo-Mexican-American relations in southern California. The formation of such programs throughout the Southwest, Texas, and California did not serve a purely academic purpose. Rather it attempted to force the individual Mexican-Americans into a homogeneous mold. These programs simplistically took student discontent, argued that Mexican-American students were discriminated against educationally because they were Mexicans, and created support for boondoggle programs aimed not at furthering knowledge but at using the lecture hall and seminar room as centers for political agitation. In a pure form these potential malcontents received a line of training that emphasized how society had failed to give them any opportunity. Any anti-social act they might commit resulted from the rotten society and not from their individual perversity.

Chicano students, as a result, constantly receive a barrage of propaganda about how they must subsume their individuality to the larger cause of *la raza*. Chicanos view themselves as a new breed, a mestizo product; yet, the cultural *mestizaje* that occurred in Mexico also blended with the Anglo to produce a value system within the Mexican-American community that is itself hybridized. Therefore, rejection of Anglo values by the Chicanos is really a rejection of one element of the Chicano culture. Yet, the academic advocates of *chicanismo* constantly point out the Indian heritage of the Mexican-American. They refuse to deal with cultural hybridization for fear that it might negate the purity of the mythical Indian background.

The rip-off of academia by the academics also spread into the barrios. Mexican-American students were ultimately convinced that society had robbed them. Students told non-student Chicanos that their problems were based on the inequities of the larger society that consciously discriminated against anyone that was different. Thus, riots occurred, feelings polarized, and amicable solutions to outstanding and very real problems were retarded.

Sister Maureen! There are Mexicans in the Church!

Cultural
Schizophrenia

Recent onslaughts of ethnicity and minority group consciousness forced the academic community into a recognition of the existence of groups traditionally ignored by researchers in the social sciences and the humanities. Motivation for such recognition emerged not so much from genuine concern as from the penitential thrust to atone for sins of the past. Consequently, the traditional approaches to academic research suffered from the rush to make the study of ethnic groups—Blacks, Mexican-Americans, Native Americans,—relevant. Given the virginal character of Mexican-American history, the researcher needs to study the Mexican-American within the

153

context of both the United States and the cultural matrix of Mexico.

Areas of cultural transference from Mexico to the Mexican-American enclaves in the United States need careful and detailed examination. Political institutions, religious practices, socio-economic determinants, and cultural values inherent within Mexican and United States society bear scrutiny. Of necessity, the cultural conflict between Mexicans recently arrived in the United States and the dominant culture require study. Of greatest import, however, is the imperative of historical perspective to the Mexican-American in order to evaluate better the current situation confronting that group.

A pattern of cultural conflict emerged by 1900. Subsequent events in both the United States and Mexico presaged an increase in cultural tension in the former Spanish borderlands. Patterns of behavior would be brought into cultural relations as an area of potential disagreement, violence, and distrust.

After the inception of the Mexican Revolution in 1910, more Mexican social and cultural institutions were transferred into the Spanish borderlands as more Mexicans moved into the United States and mingled with extant Spanish-speaking groups. Such institutional transfers, in all probability, punctuated the tensions between the essentially Anglo-Protestant and the Mexican-Catholic groups of the area. Anglo tendencies to lump together all Mexican-Americans clearly indicated the ignorance and lack of perceptivity by members of the dominant culture. The Mexican-American and the more recently arrived immigrants from Mexico composed a heterogeneous social group. All members of Mexico's social strata were represented. Only a portion of this group ended up in the urban barrios, or agricultural workers' enclaves, throughout the Southwest. Yet, the Anglo tendency to group the Mexican-American into a stereotyped barrio dweller or migratory farm laborer blurred the distinctions within the Mexican-American subculture.

The present-day Mexican-American apparently differs very little from his antecedents, especially at the lower social strata. Ethnic focal values, i.e., familial ties, machismo, *envidia* ("envy"), and *compadrazgo* ("godfather relationship"), find their strongest and most tenacious refuge in the lower classes. The persistence of these values grew out of a folk culture that centered upon the rural life of northern Mexico.

While folk culture dominates the lower levels of Mexican-American society, as Mexican-Americans achieved higher social and economic positions they acquired greater class consciousness. They became aware of marked differences between themselves and their less fortunate *carnales* ("soul brothers") of the barrios in major Southwestern cities. These more economically mobile Mexican-Americans perceived with greater perspicacity the difference within the Mexican-American social milieu. A clear transfer of a stratified social institution from Mexico occurred. Members of the Mexican-American community recognized the existence of a pecking order within their own society. Yet, as a Mexican-American middle and upper class became more class conscious, it also adopted more of the *mores* of the dominant Anglo group.

As some Mexican-Americans increased in affluence and became more perceptive about social distinctions, some of the more cohesive elements of the Mexican-American family began to disintegrate. Strong familial ties, both to a nuclear and extended family, weakened as second and third generations of Mexican-Americans worked their way up the socio-economic ladder. Meanwhile, back at the barrio, these escapees from the barrio culture received the onus of traitors to their people. What occurred was an incompatability of value systems. The younger Mexican-Americans desired a change in their lives uninhibited by a recalcitrant family. Older family members remaining in ethnic enclaves, on the other hand, saw the destruction as a serious threat to fundamental social values.

Again, institutional transfer occurred from Mexico. Since the Spanish conquest of New Spain, the family unit acted as the cohesive element of society. In villages and larger urban areas, the ties of blood and marriage superseded any other allegiance. Increased urbanization, however, posed a threat to the strong family structure, and consequently, a breakup occurred. Likewise, as Mexicans moved to the United States and began to settle in cities in increasing numbers, the more socially ambitious attempted to break away from the old patterns that offered their parents and grandparents security in an alien land.

Yet, not all of the old values received rejection by socially mobile Mexican-Americans. Much of the ceremonial aspect of Mexican life remained a viable element of Mexican-American society at all levels. Individual deportment mandated that a man conduct himself with *dignidad,* or dignity. He must act as himself without the self-effacing camaraderie of the Anglo. To the Mexican-American who clung to much of the formality of his society, the boisterousness of the Anglo strikes him as bad taste and as a clear negation of individual presence and bearing.

Such individual insularity and aloofness came about because the Mexican attempted to come to grips with his own cultural identity. The violent seizure of Mexico by Spain produced a cultural schizophrenia. The Mexican viewed himself as neither Spaniard nor Indian; such a cultural schism forced him into a solitude where he could never reveal his innermost feelings for fear of losing what he considered a precarious social equilibrium. Consequently, the Mexican wrapped himself in a robe of *dignidad,* breaking loose occasionally when sufficient alcohol permitted a release of inhibitions. Concomitant with such aloofness came an endemic *desconfianza,* or lack of trust, in institutions in general. The Mexican trusted no one except himself, and even then he was aware of his fallibility.

The very aloofness that is considered de rigueur for the Mexican or Mexican-American male also forced them into other associations similar to social institutions in Mexico. Usually male socialization occurred along bilateral kinship lines. One joined with cousins, *compadres* ("godfathers"), in-laws, and other members of an extended family rather than with associations outside of these social contacts. At differing age levels, young men formed *palomillas,* or gangs, composed again of members of a broadly extended family. Women of this extended family, however, maintained a more cloistered closeness and counsel in matters ranging from disease to social relations outside the family.

Mexican folk culture and its concept of disease transferred to the borderlands when immigrants from Mexico migrated to the United States. In one city in the Southwest, a land development company bought lands in the lower Rio Grande Valley and precipitated a migratory wave of Anglos and Mexicans to occupy the area. Nine thousand Mexicans from isolated ranchos in northern Mexico transplanted their traditions in Mecca, Hidalgo County, Texas. Traditional concepts of disease transferred across the Rio Grande and became an integral part of the new Mexican-American community in Mecca. *Males naturales,* or acts of God, included a variety of intestinal disorders, hysteria, or fright, and *caída de la mollera,* or collapsed fontanel, in infants. *Males artificiales,* or illness created by man, became a different problem. *Mal puesto,* or sorcery, and *mal de ojo,* or evil eye, required the intervention of a *curandero,* a quasi-medicine man prevalent in most rural Mexican communities.

Such a cultural transfer reached ridiculous extremes. Popular medical mythology among Mexican-Americans declared that these diseases could not be cured by a physician, be he Mexican, Anglo, or Mexican-American. Ancient traditions needed to be invoked against these persistent maladies to which only Mexican-Americans were susceptible. In Mecca, Texas, as social mobility infiltrated the Mexican population of that community, the more affluent Mexican-Americans viewed such superstition as pure bunk. Such a negation of traditional values caused anxiety within the total Mexican-American community for fear that the heretics might become afflicted by a perturbed *curandero*.

Another medical concept to intrude itself into the Mexican-American communities was the persistance of the *curandero*. These individuals possessed a great deal of influence within the traditional confines of the community. They usually wielded influence as a result of a confidence in their own mission within the society. This charismatic influence resembled the power of caciques and caudillos in Mexico itself. These individuals, through a complex nexus of personal and family alliances coupled with their own personal magnetism, controlled sufficient power to lead whole areas into revolt or in support of a government or movement.

The heterogeneity of the Mexican-American communities throughout California and the Southwest resulted in inter-barrio tensions growing out of difference in relative social positions of the inhabitants. Not unlike barrio rivalries in Mexican villages, members of Mexican-American barrios confined their social contacts to local areas and the resultant social relations within them. Barrio competition engendered a fierce loyalty from the population. In this regard, the *patria chica* concept that kept Mexican villagers intensely loyal to their local areas instead of an inchoate nation became an integral factor in the organization of Mexican-American enclaves.

The *patria chica* applies as well to certain rural occupations of Mexican-Americans. Mexican vaqueros employed by the King ranch in South Texas held the ranch up as a primary unit of citizenship. The King vaquero referred to himself as a *kiñeno* in the same way that a person from Nogales, Sonora, refers to himself as a *nogalense*.

Transference of social patterns and institutions to the Southwest and California before 1940 can be divided roughly between rural and urban areas. By the early 1960's, eighty percent of Mexican-Americans occupied urban areas. In Los Angeles and Long Beach, there are more Mexicans than in any other city with the exception of Mexico City.

Increased urbanization precipitated a mass movement out of barrio culture. More established Mexican-Americans moved out of traditional neighborhoods as new arrivals from Mexico clamored for space. Urbanization consequently helped the socially ambitious achieve the mobility they sought.

Prior to the 1940s, Mexican-American concentrations in southwestern cities contained substantial elements of middle- and upper-class refugees who fled from the internal strife of Mexico's chaotic revolutionary period. Generally, these groups considered themselves exiles merely awaiting an opportunity to go back to Mexico. They formed political groups that attempted to lobby for their faction in the United States. These loosely joined political conglomerations roughly paralleled the political factions that sought power in Mexico between 1910 and 1930. During that time, even the most illiterate refugee maintained an interest in the political developments south of the Rio Grande.

Since the first waves of refugees arrived in the Southwest after 1910, the Mexican-Americans maintained a romantic desire to return to the *patria*. Some evidence exists for the idea that the emotional attachment persisted for one's native state in Mexico rather than the nation. In Los Angeles, for example, the barrios were often organized along state lines and maintained social clubs and athletic organizations for those of state affiliations.

While loyalty to the *patria* remained a romantic ideal, a more practical loyalty possesses the Mexican-American. Although functional bilingualism accelerated in the Mexican-American population, there persisted a strong attachment to the use of Spanish as a means of preserving the mother culture.

Language gave to the Mexican-American a cultural cohesiveness that could not be disrupted by social mobility, the introduction of new arrivals from Mexico, and the general press of urban life after 1940. While at variance with an urban milieu, the language united disparate Mexican-Americans from all social strata. In fact, ethnic values stressing material achievement seem far less tenacious than the hold of language on the Mexican-American.

Mexican-American society and all of its cultural ramifications remain essentially a carbon copy of social practices introduced from Mexico. While remaining more pristine in the traditionally oriented lower classes, certain values, such as language, act as a force for unity. There is, however, a breakdown of traditional values as a Mexican-American moves upward. Familial ties weaken; language, while remaining a force, yields to bilingualism. On occasion, Spanish is replaced by English. With this replacement comes a greater emphasis on Anglo values, such as a work ethic, that tends to dilute the Mexican-American culture.

One area of social and cultural concern for the Mexican-American requires individual treatment: namely, the influence of religion upon the Mexican-American. Religious practices reaching the United States from Mexico came into conflict with values adopted by Anglo, Irish, Polish, and Italian Catholics and caused substantial conflict as Mexicans crowded into the urban centers and rural areas of the Southwest.

Religion in Mexico plays a strong role in the society despite official strictures against the Roman Catholic Church. The Mexican Constitution of 1917 struck a particularly anti-clerical note when it destroyed the Church's right to hold property and to teach religion within its regular school curricula. Yet, the restrictions imposed upon the Church failed to diminish the nearly mystical piety of the general population. In some respects, official censure of the Church probably strengthened individual devotion through the limitation upon the number of priests in each Mexican state. The paucity of priests meant that communication with God must be an individual effort, performed without benefit of clergy.

Mexican religious practices emphasize the ceremonial and personalistic side of faith. In Mexican villages and in barrios in Mexican cities, parish churches achieve a completeness of character. Local patron saints are venerated not merely as intercessors between God and the supplicant, but as beings endowed with their own power to grant supplications. The concept of a universality of faith rarely becomes a matter of discussion in Mexico. Instead, fiestas are organized for religious holidays and for local saint's days. The Church, in short, serves as an element of social significance within the Mexican society. In addition, individual piety becomes a key to Mexican religion. A religious fatalism invades the Mexican and grants to him a sense of resignation. The will of God often becomes the explanation for events and personal tragedies.

Religious practices from Mexico were never introduced into California and the Southwest. Instead, they were an integral part of the area before the United States takeover in 1848. Subsequent to that event the Roman Catholic Church in the Southwest never received the impetus of Americanization that occurred in the East and the Midwest. The clerics who ministered to clusters of the faithful literally were padres on horseback, irregularly administering the sacraments and tending to the pastoral needs of their far flung communicants.

As a consequence, the individual piety so prevalent in Mexico also characterized the religious life of the Mexican-American. In the isolated mountain villages of northern New Mexico, for example, one observer described the resigned religious quality of the Hispano inhabitants of that area. One man, she observed, had a daughter who suffered from a prolonged illness. When she died, the man declared that "she no longer suffers. God has taken her."

The essentially Mexican character of Roman Catholicism in the Southwest and California prompted action in the Archdiocese of Los Angeles between 1920 and 1949. The Church in Los Angeles sought to Americanize the Mexican-American. In part, this action resulted from a desire to assist the newly arrived immigrants to adapt to the new society and culture of the United States. Not only in Los Angeles but in the Southwest the Church strove to grasp the Mexican-American and break the grip of folk culture. The intensified efforts to educate the Mexican-American in the essentials of Roman Catholic doctrine placed a great strain upon the resources of the Church in California and the Southwest. The Church found itself at a disadvantage, for most of the immigrants between 1910 and 1950 came from rural areas where irregular priestly visitations comprised formal religious observances. Instead, folk culture and individual piety filled the spiritual vacuum.

While pastoral concerns occupied the Church between 1910-1950, subsequent decades saw a turn in emphasis. Between 1949 and 1967, the Archdiocese of Los Angeles, dominated by an Irish hierarchy, intensified its efforts to Americanize the Mexican-American. A school building frenzy struck the Archdiocese. Bricks were laid. Parishioners coughed up dollars, and as a result, by 1960, practically every parish in East Los Angeles, one of the heaviest concentrations of Mexican-Americans in California, possessed a parochial school that not only taught a general curriculum and religious instruction but also aimed at the acculturation of its parishioners.

Attempts to Americanize the Mexican-American in Los Angeles did not have unanimous support. In 1947, two years before the intensified school building program began, an anonymous letter was addressed to Pope Pius XII. Probably written by a priest of Mexican extraction, the memorandum entitled "'Religious Assistance to the Mexican People in the United States" outlined four factors that plagued such help to the Mexican-American. First, the anonymous author noted psychological racial differences between the Anglo and the Mexican. Secondly, linguistic barriers would inevitably hamper religious and cultural homogenization. Penultimately, the Mexicans possessed a strong attachment to their religious heritage and would be loath to make changes in their popular traditions. Finally, the Anglo desired to Americanize ethnic groups residing in the United States in the hope of forcing some cultural homogeneity. Such a warning presaged the conflict between Anglo and Mexican-American cultures in the 1960s.

The Church, however, remained steadfast in the pursuit of its twin goals. It must first preserve the Faith for the Mexican-Americans and keep Protestantism from gaining a foothold. In an equal sense, however, the Church struggled against the accusations that it was an agent of Rome. It wanted to demonstrate to the larger society that it could Americanize its Mexican laity as a patriotic act.

The urban Church in California was not the only object of priestly concern. Migrant laborers throughout the Southwest and the San Joaquin and Imperial valleys of California suffered from pastoral neglect. In 1949, priests began to receive extradiocesan assignments to minister to migrant Mexican laborers in California. By 1960, however, these peripatetic clerics became socially oriented and incurred the anger of wealthy Catholic farmers. The recalling of these extradiocesan pastors probably resulted from pressures brought to bear upon the ecclesiastical hierarchy by wealthy rural communicants. In addition, the termination of the bracero program in 1965 reduced the number of migrant laborers, the raison d'etre of the entire program.

Social activism in the late 1950s and early 1960s replaced the strictly pastoral concerns of the Church in the Southwest and California. Priestly involvement in the Delano grape strike and in the strike of agricultural workers in Brownsville, Texas, in 1966, indicated that the priests operated in a milieu of social protest. Even the ecclesiastical hierarchy, generally cautious and conservative, recognized the social pressures that catapulted the Mexican-American into prominence as a potential force.

In San Antonio, Texas, the Bishop in 1945 secured the creation of a Bishop's Committee for the Spanish speaking. Gradually, cautiously, the Committee evolved from a pastoral group into one that supported moderate social reform. In the 1960s, the Bishop's Committee came out in favor of the right of agricultural labor to unionize.

Socially motivated clergy gave impetus to the transfer of the *cursillo* (short course) movement from Spain in 1957. It attracted individuals who sought religious renewal and dedication. The *cursillo* program drew an action-oriented clergy and laity. For three days, the *cursillistas* received "techniques of group dynamics and old fashioned frontier revival."

The present state of the Church and the Mexican-American continues unresolved. Real problems persist. The Church failed to make inroads in its bent for Americanization, and, as a consequence, it helped alienate those with a formal allegiance to it as an institution. Mexican-American attendance at Mass proved low. There also occurred a decrease in church marriages among Mexican-Americans. In part, this could be explained by the Mexican tradition of a civil ceremony as being the only legitimate one recognized by the state. Moreover, the socialization of Mexican-American Catholics failed in that the hoped-for Catholic homogenization did not materialize. Church lay groups with an Anglo or Irish bent could not attract Mexican-American parishioners, and few attempts were made by the clergy to draw the Mexican-American on his cultural terms. A high degree of personal piety exists, however, within the Mexican-American community despite the low attendance figures at Mass.

The political tradition inherited from Mexico constituted one element of Mexican-American cultural values that acted both as hindrance and as an asset to residents of the barrios and the small villages throughout the Southwest. Local caciques, or bosses, manipulated their alliances with other powerful members of a village and exercised virtual control over the area. Often these unions resulted from familial ties, often *compadrazgo* played a role, and at times wealth elevated an individual to power within a village. Like religion, *caciquismo* did not transfer to the Southwest and California. Its existence in that area predated the arrival of the Anglos by two hundred years.

Throughout Spain's far-flung empire in North America conquistadores and colonizers controlled indigenous groups through the incorporation of Indian leaders into the Spanish system of government. Such a union of Indian and Spanish leadership led to the perpetuation of a cacique class that later became controlled by mestizos. In part, the hold of the cacique predicated itself upon the relative geographic isolation between the disparate villages and the administrative hub in Mexico City. Virtually semi-autonomous, caciques in the Southwest governed villages through an intricate system of alliances.

In the evolution of a cacique system in Mexico and the Southwest, a transmutation of the concept of nobility also occurred. The *don*, a title of respect generally applied to the Spanish gentry and to the Indian nobility that became integrated into the Spanish system, gradually achieved applicability to any powerful individual in a village who possessed some political influence. As such, the phenomenon of "donship" became an integral part of the political milieu encountered by the Anglos when they reached Spanish and Mexican territories and later acquired them in 1848.

As the nineteenth century waned, the immigration that

augmented the Spanish-speaking population of the Southwest reinforced the "donship" concept. Traditional "donship" revolved around the *patrón,* or employer. This relationship had its roots in the widely scattered haciendas of northern
Mexico and was predicated upon an interdependence between
the *patrón* and his workers. Mexican immigrants entering the
Southwest served to strengthen the cultural significance of the
don as they moved into extant Mexican-American enclaves.

The *patrón,* however, was but one element of "donship."
In the United States Southwest the Mexican consul at various
cities also received the title, both out of respect for the office
and for the personal qualities of the individual. Along with the
Mexican consul, wealthy Mexican-American businessmen
were granted the designation. Politically, the descendants of
the cacique tradition were referred to as *dones.* This perpetuation of a tradition indigenous to the New World and incorporated into Spanish rule set apart some of the Mexican-
American communities. Moreover, respected *curanderos,*
because of their great power, were usually referred to as *don.*
Given the patriarchal nature of Mexican society, old men were
venerated with the title *don.*

The Mexican-American cultural phenomenon of "donship" profoundly though subtly affected the evolution of
Mexican-American political organizations. As early as the turn
of the century some attempts appeared to organize Mexican
residents of the United States into ethnic political clubs in
order to give them greater public influence. In the 1920s, the
League of Latin American Citizens (LULAC) undertook as a
conscious effort to integrate Mexican-Americans into the
United States political system. LULAC required that its members speak functional English as a means of assuring a greater
awareness of political phenomena.

Subsequent developments in the 1950s and 1960s saw the
emergence of more militant and nationalistic Mexican-
American political organizations. Groups such as the

Mexican-American Political Association (MAPA), the Political Association of Spanish Speaking Organizations (PASSO), the Community Service Organization (CSO), and lately the American GI Forum consciously strove to develop an awareness among Mexican-Americans of a cultural identity and of their potential as a political force. Consequently, they did not mandate English as a prerequisite for membership.

More recent Mexican-American political groups differed from each other only in degree. The principal aim of these groups remained the election of their own people to political power. For example, PASSO and MAPA differ in the emphasis that they place on alliance with other ethnic organizations. MAPA chose to remain blatantly Mexican while PASSO moved to alliance with Blacks and Puerto Ricans in an attempt to garner political power and influence. In addition, organizations such as the CSO and the American GI Forum aimed at political education among Mexican-Americans in order to increase voter registration.

An odd contradiction, probably more apparent than real, within all Mexican-American organizations is the rhetoric of loyalty to the United States. At the same time, they declare themselves on the basis of historical primacy. The "we were here first" idea, based upon Spanish and Mexican occupation of the Southwest and California, is a declaration of cultural uniqueness and of antipathy to the Anglo takeover of former Mexican areas.

Principal among the problems of Mexican-American political organizations is the split between more moderate elements and those that cry out for total political power and influence. Social action, of late, has become the most insistent aspect of organizations like PASSO and MAPA. Even LULAC and the American GI Forum, both reasonably conservative groups, became involved in the beginnings of social action programs working through federal agencies such as the Office of Economic Opportunity.

With the exception of infusions of federal monies into social action programs, the Mexican-Ámerican political organizations still suffer from a lack of funding. They have failed to make money-raising a sophisticated art, and financial support remains haphazard. In 1968, however, the Ford Foundation granted the sum of $2.2 million for the establishment of a Legal Defense and Education Fund for the Mexican-Americans of the Southwest. It followed the legal model of a comparable group within the National Association of Colored People (NAACP). The Foundation granted monies for the legal education of minority group members and finally supported the formation of a Southwest Council of La Raza.

Within the political system of the United States, however the Mexican-American remained tied to the Democratic Party. Such a tenacious allegiance hampers organizational effectiveness among Mexican-Americans, for members of Democratic and occasionally Republican clubs also belong to ethnic political clubs. As a consequence, membership is duplicative and support remains narrowly based.

Mexican-American political leaders also face problems of validation of their leadership. To become acceptable leaders of their group they need the acceptance of the dominant Anglo community. Yet, they cannot appear as *vendidos*. They must have a command of English, be elected to office by both Anglos and Mexican-Americans, and remain essentially loyal to the interests of their ethnic group without being rejected by the Anglo. In short, they perch precariously on a political tightrope. Moreover, leadership fragmentation and parochialism militate against the emergence of a regionally acceptable political leadership among the Mexican-Americans.

The political system which the Mexican-American operates and the apparent disunity among the diverse Mexican-American groups work against political effectiveness. The gerrymandering of political districts throughout the Southwest costs the Mexican-Americans influence in the marshalling of votes. Internal political juggling by Anglo political

machinery consequently receives reinforcement from unso-
phisticated migrants from rural areas who move into urban
districts. Finally, the low naturalization rate among Mexican
citizens reduces the political effectiveness of Mexicans residing
in the United States.

The Mexican-American, therefore, possesses little
"political clout." Unlike the Black, no one ostensibly fought a
war over them nor were they enslaved. The Mexican-American
lacks a central form of organization that would coordinate disparate activities and grant them a more effective, channeled
political voice.

The Mexican-American began on a traditional Mexican
political base. *Dones* and caciques wielded a powerful influence over the political destinies of a vast population. Yet, in
the recent past, increased Mexican-American political activity
forced an adoption of Anglo political values and systems in
order to maintain a precarious effectiveness. This "working
within the system" did not, however, have unanimous support from all Mexican-Americans. Militancy grew in the 1960s
and sought to polarize Mexican-American culture and politics.

A nationalist movement is afoot in the United States that
possesses traditions predating the arrival of settlers in Virginia
in 1607. The Mexican-American discovered a sense of nationality somewhat removed from an allegiance to the predominantly Anglo culture of the United States. Yet, the movement
has failed to grip the majority of Mexican-Americans, many of
whom settled comfortably into the Anglo society that ultimately accepted them. To the militant Mexican-American, the
act of acceptance by the Anglo society symbolized a rejection of
autochthonous culture by the Mexican-American. In so doing,
he became labeled with the pejorative of *Tío Taco* or *Vendido*.

In part, the lack of cohesion in the recrudescent Mexican-
American nationalism emerged from the very differences
within the Mexican-American community. While language
acted as a force for maintaining contact among the disparate
elements of that group, semantic disagreements also separated

its various elements. Essentially, the Mexican-American disagreed over what exactly their ethnicity entailed. Were they "Spanish-speaking," Mexican-Americans, Latin Americans, Hispanos, Chicanos? The degree of adherence to one particular sobriquet clearly indicated the view of the individual toward the dominant Anglo society and toward the emergent Mexican-American movement.

To the militant, the term Chicano, formerly a pejorative applied to Mexicans in general, became a symbol of uniqueness from the Anglo society. In March, 1969, at the First National Chicano Youth Liberation Conference held in Denver, Colorado, the delegates presented the *Plan Espiritual de Aztlán*. The document declared the solidarity of the Chicano people. It drew, in part, from the *raza cósmica* idea presented by the Mexican philosopher José Vasconcelos wherein he saw a solidarity between the mestizo peoples of the Western Hemisphere. The very name Aztlán was the Nahuatl or Aztec term for what is now the Southwest. In this declaration *indigenista* elements emerged to extoll the Indian over the Spanish side of Mexican-American and Mexican culture. It was, in short, a carry over from the *indigenista* "binge" in which Mexico indulges sporadically.

The *Plan Espiritual de Aztlán* railed against the brutal gringo invaders of the *patria*. In a declaration of historical primacy, the *Plan* laid principal claim to the Southwest. Its call was nationalistic, extolling the existence of a Chicano nation. The Chicano goals, as enunciated in the *Plan de Aztlán*, were clearly activist. It demanded a mass commitment to Chicano control of their own economic lives and education. Because of the essentially racist tendencies of Anglo society, the Chicano would have to defend his own community. Cultural values of *la raza*, declared the *Plan*, such as family and home would "prove as a powerful weapon to defeat the gringo dollar value system. . . ." It also decried working within the two-party system.

Such a commitment to traditional values and such a rejection of the dominant Anglo culture clearly emerged as an attempt to set the Chicano apart from the society in which he resided. The use of a political plan became a symbolic act of retreat to the Mexican expedient. The call for social values of the family and the home again reaffirmed tradition. Implicit within such a familial retreat was *compadrazgo*. All Chicanos were *compadres*. Each committed himself to a betterment of *la raza*. *Chicanismo* based itself upon the individual's awareness of his culture and upon the responsibilities inherent in *compadrazgo*.

Some Mexican-Americans, however, recognized the reality of existence within the Southwest. A more moderate position was enunciated before the United States Congress on February 26, 1970, when a declaration for cultural pluralism was made.

Rodolfo "Corky" González, the Chicano leader of Denver, Colorado, recognized extant political realities. Though a Chicano nationalist, he, nonetheless, saw that only through effective political organization could the Mexican-American exert a powerful influence on his own life and political destiny. To achieve this, González advocated the nationalist pride of being a Chicano. *La raza*, to González, was a large family in which its individual members had pride. He declared: "Liberation comes from self-determination. . . ." This, however, could only emerge when the Mexican-Americans took pride in their existence.

Political and cultural militancy made itself felt in predominantly Mexican-American schools throughout the Southwest and California. In Texas, for example, Mexican-American students argued that they suffered from discrimination because of their ethnic background. They demanded college preparatory classes, counseling on academic matters, financial assistance and grants, and equal opportunity to attempt things other than industrial arts and home economics. In one instance a teacher wanted to know what the turmoil was all about. The teacher declared: "You're all Americans." One girl responded with a strident negation: "I am a Mexican-American." A sense of Brown pride manifested itself. The girl cited the example of the Virgin of Guadalupe appearing as a brown virgin to an Indian boy on December 12, 1531.

Militancy in the schools throughout the Southwest and California resulted in an increase of emphasis upon the Mexican-American as a cultural entity. Chicano militants successfully brought about curricular changes in various cities throughout the land of Aztlán. In one example, Crystal City, Texas, Mexican-Americans swept the school board elections on April 4, 1970. The school board takeover resulted from a joint political effort between the Mexican-American Youth Organization (MAYO) and the *Raza Unida* Party of Crystal City. Voter registration drives on the part of the *Raza Unida* workers brought Mexican-Americans to the polls and gave the *Raza Unida* Party a resounding victory.

Chicano militancy, while strident and disruptive, addressed itself to specific issues. A prime example of this is the land grant controversy, still unresolved, in which Reies López Tijerina emerged as the spokesman for the *Alianza Federal de los Pueblos Libres*. López Tijerina and his followers have consistently argued that the Treaty of Guadalupe Hidalgo of 1848 that granted New Mexico to the United States guaranteed the protection of extant Mexican lands and Mexican culture. The gradual dispossession of New Mexicans by both private and public forces became the focal point of the struggle. Violence as well as litigation have characterized the long struggle for a restitution of allegedly alienated lands.

Another long, grueling problem that was temporarily settled in 1968 appeared in the grape strike in Delano, California. Essentially a labor-management dispute, the strike became a focal point of Chicano activism. In addition, Anglo sympathizers as well as ecclesiastical supporters declared for

César Estrada Chávez and his union. Political leaders scurried to be photographed with Chávez. Establishment liberals sang his praises at cocktail parties and supported his boycott of stores that continued to sell table grapes. Chávez and his supporters used traditional labor tactics to achieve their ends. The major variant, however, was the ethnic overtone given to the strike. César Chávez soon took on characteristics of Benito Juárez, Emiliano Zapata, and Pancho Villa. Chávez as the charismatic caudillo operated in a milieu of labor-mangement relations and ultimately succeeded in gaining labor contracts for his union.

The Chávez grape strike became a symbol of one element of the Mexican-American population in California and the Southwest. His movement generated a cultural boom spearheaded by Luis Miguel Valdez. Valdez founded the *Teatro Campesino* ("Country Theater") in Del Rey, California. Valdez, a poet, occasional college teacher, and alumnus of the San Francisco Mime Theater, saw in the grape strike a chance for Mexican-American culture to achieve a renascence. To Valdez, the Mexican-Americans need an organized cultural tradition in order to articulate their needs. The *Teatro Campesino* provides an outlet for cultural experimentation. Moreover, it is based upon old Spanish traditions but set in the context of migrant labor in the United States, and its productions are part morality plays or worker theater. The staff of the *Teatro Campesino* is composed wholly of agricultural workers. Agustín Lira, a grape picker, is the resident guitarist and poet and writes *corridos,* based on the Mexican folk songs, about the migrant laborers in the agricultural belt of California. Through Valdez' inspiration, other Chicano theaters emerged in the Southwest in an attempt to find an autochthonous art style for *la raza.*

Literature on the Mexican-American, while losing some of the stridency of the 1960s, has still failed to produce a work of major significance. One work I recommend, however, written

by an Anglo, is John Nichols' *Milagro Bean Field War*. This
book is a delight. It is set in what is obviously New Mexico and
deals with an aspect of the land grant dispute. Despite the come-
dic undertone of the work, Nichols deals with a tremendously
complex problem in a humane and sensitive way. He clearly de-
monstrates the mixed nature of the support for and against the
various factions in the land problems in northern New Mexico.
He shows Anglos and Hispanos on both sides of the issues. At
the same time, he depicts his characters as essentially human,
mixing good and evil in pretty even doses. Nichols' work deserves attention, and it can also be appreciated as a good tale that
makes you want to laugh and cry at the same time.

Mexican-American militancy aimed at both political and
cultural birth. Through the medium of politics, Chicano
militants hoped to achieve power and a sense of separation
from the dominant Anglo culture. At the same time a sense of
nationalism and pride in one's *chicanismo* has manifested itself among the militant Mexican-Americans. The militant
pride, however, circumscribes certain elements of Mexican culture. Iberian influences are denigrated and the barbarities of
the Aztecs are upheld. Such an unhistorical position perpetuates a perverse *indigenismo* that tends to alienate moderate
and conservative Mexican-Americans and thus to weaken the
thrust for solidarity.

Despite the militant upsurge, the Mexican-American
remains a heterogeneous social group composed of varying
social strata and possessing disparate aspirations. Popular
attempts at cultural homogeneity tend to disregard the tri-
partite nature of the Mexican-American. Indian and Spanish
elements blended to produce a Mexican that shared both cultures. With the transference of the Southwest to the United
States, the Anglo culture infiltrated an essentially Mexican
one. As a consequence, Mexican-Americans who aspired to
social betterment adopted, at least superficially, some of the
dominant *mores* of their Anglo countrymen. The result of such

an adaptation was the abandonment of·traditional cultural values as the Mexican-American moved out of the barrio and the rural villages.

The militant, however, claimed a homogeneity that rejected Anglo values entirely. Chauvinistic elements attempted to arouse an entire people against their fellow citizens. While some Mexican-American organizations sought to work within an extant political and social system and at the same time disseminate pride in their Mexican heritage, others became stridently militant. In their militancy, they alienated moderate Mexican-Americans who had succeeded within the dominant political and social system. Congressman Henry B. González of San Antonio, Texas, perhaps put it best: "I am against hate and the spreaders of hate. . . ."

10

A Summing Up

If nothing else, the history of the Mexican-American clearly indicates a great need for further research devoid of ideological and ethnic considerations. Not a great deal can be accomplished with the polarization that now sets off one group against the other. The polarity—both academic and political—makes for an uncomfortable situation for any researcher who does not want to be hassled by militants and reactionaries alike.

177

A good example of this sort of historical misunderstanding in the general society emerges on television, in newspapers, and national magazines. Just imagine a not-too-long-ago situation. The silver screen in the living room just announced finis to a program. Now the sponsors have a chance to hawk their product so that a gullible, T.V.-hypnotized public will increase corporate profits. A food company, Frito-Lay, comes on the air. As the commercial begins, one hears: "Ay, ay, ay, ay, I am the Frito-Bandito; I love Frito Corn Cheeps, I love them I do, the Frito-Bandito will steal them from you!!" Visually a short, chunky, sombreroed, and mustachioed little Mexican type bearing a brace of pistols is apprehended in the process of lifting this delectable food. No longer do we see the Frito Bandito on the tube. Militant Chicanos took umbrage at the stereotype that the Frito-Lay Company used in pushing one of their many food products. It was claimed that the Frito Bandito denigrated their Mexican heritage by presenting a stereotype who was dishonest and constantly busted by the Anglo fuzz. From one point of view, they are right, considering that the Age of Aquarius has become the Age of the Uptight and the Righteous.

The impasse between Frito-Lay and the militant Chicanos typifies the mutual historical ignorance of Anglo and Mexican-American cultures. Moderate Mexican-Americans dismissed the Frito Bandito as merely *una cosa de los gringos incultos* ("a thing of the uncultured gringos") and went about their day-to-day affairs. Certainly any perspicacious Mexican knows that the Anglo liberal, especially those of academic vocation, must be tolerated and pitied. Unfortunately, reasonable. Anglos and moderate Mexican-Americans, both in the majority, fail to have the time to devote to historical studies in any sort of profound way. Instead, unless they are active academicians, they are otherwise too busy earning a living and coping with the pressures of modern society to worry about the historical implications of a funny little guy in a straw hat who is crazy about Fritos.

As the 1960s clearly indicated, the Mexican-American increased in political importance. As a result he needed to be studied, dissected, analyzed, and generally subjected to scrutiny by swarms of academic pathologists. Academicians and bleeding heart liberals, terms that often interchange without a substantive loss of meaning, step into the breach and begin a minute, preconceived analysis of the Mexican-American. Now that the Mexican-American has become a problem, he needs a variety of governmental agencies to make him a better American. In short, he must be transformed. The Puritan work ethic in its most denatured form must be shoved down the Mexican-American's throat along with his tortillas and frijoles.

In its broadest implications, the prevalent attitude vis-à-vis the Mexican-American is to leap into the present with him rather than study his historical evolution. Self-flagellating academicians and professional do-gooders thrive upon the postulation of ideas upon the vacuum of the present rather than upon the experience of the past. While admittedly historical studies do not serve the crystal ball gazer and resident prognosticator, they do give a cultural frame of reference to the study of the Mexican-American.

One outstanding example of the sort of pigeonholing that has occurred is the lumping of the Mexican-American as a part of the Third World. It is to say that Africa, Asia, and Latin America, along with the former Mexican territories of the United States, share common cultural roots and therefore developed along similar lines. This is not analysis but rather the imposition of an ideological framework upon the Mexican-American experience. It is, in essence, the acceptance of the Third World concept, a basically Anglo intellectual phenomenon, as an excuse to avoid nitty-gritty research and study.

The formation of Chicano studies programs occurred along ideological lines. They became a means by which Chicanos who were insecure about their Mexican-American background could find ready countermyths to those prevalent in the greater society. Chicano fantasy became the crux of

Chicano studies. One of these fantasies was that only a Chicano could teach Chicano studies. Perhaps this is true if one wants only to deal with pure emotions, and if one wants to ignore judicious analysis of data and the making of considered judgments. But to say that only a Chicano can teach Chicano history is to wallow in ethnic absurdity.

An analogous situation emerged in the fall of 1974. A popular television program made its debut at that time and soon shot to the top of the charts. The program, "Chico and the Man" starred Jack Albertson and a newcomer, Freddy Prinz. Unfortunately, Prinze came under considerable criticism from Chicanos because he was not a Mexican-American. Rather he was Hungarian and Puerto Rican and described himself as a Hungarican. The program served as a superb put-on. It did a fairly intelligent job of satirizing both Anglo and Mexican stereotypes. According to Prinze, "If I can't play a Chicano because I'm Puerto Rican, then God's really gonna be mad when he finds out Charlton Heston played Moses." This program, differing from other television attempts at ethnic relevance, was a sheer delight. It was genuine entertainment that also played up the necessity of individuality and of individual worth.

As we progress into the 1970s, there seems to be a trend away from some of the more absurd aspects of ethnicity. More minority students ask for studies in the more traditional academic disciplines and in different vocational programs. It took a decade for them to discover that the elements of race and culture did not open doors in the greater society. Academic tendencies toward preferential treatment for minority students is gradually abating. Academicians hate to think they are wrong; therefore, the slow restoration of higher standards for all students, minority and Anglo alike.

Politics and education joined hands in 1974 in two southwestern states. In Arizona and New Mexico, Raúl Castro and Jerry Apodaca respectively, captured the Democratic nomination in their states and were subsequently elected in November.

Both ran on tickets that strongly emphasized minority education. At the same time they did not stress preferential education, merely equality in educational opportunity.

While militant Chicanos shriek about separatism with
their *Plan de Aztlán* and the plethora of academic boon-
doggles called Chicano studies perpetuate nonsense, Castro
and Apocada emerge as true pluralists. They recognize that
social and economic integration can be achieved without a
denigration of the Mexican-American culture. In short, educational opportunity will allow Mexican-Americans to achieve
an individuality that *chicanismo* attempts to subsume.

Admittedly the Mexican-American often begins with a
language handicap. There exists a higher dropout rate of
Mexican-Americans from public schools than of any other
group. This is attributable primarily to language. In the past
teachers punished students for speaking Spanish, and their
culture was, in fact, put down. Yet, the separatism of Aztlán
fails to alleviate the problem. Instead it merely perpetuates
substandard Spanish and English. As a consequence, the
militant rank and file often fail to communicate effectively in
either language and add to their already long list of
frustrations.

The solution lies, of course, in effective bilingual education. Teachers need training in Spanish and English. Training
for students should be given in both languages. English should
not replace Spanish as a primary language but should parallel
it as a viable language and both should develop simulta-
neously. Of course a certain obstacle exists here: the orienta-
tion of Schools of Education who have primary responsibility
for the training of teachers in the United States. These bastions
of methodological mediocrity become major stumbling blocks
to any kind of change, for such innovation might threaten the
empires that they have founded with federal and state monies.
But more on this later.

It seems that, for the Mexican-American to achieve

economic and social success commensurate with his abilities, individuality must be maintained. The Mexican-American who subsumes himself to the preachments of Aztlán divests himself of one of the most outstanding characteristics of Mexican and Mexican-American culture: his individualism. By the same token Mexican-Americans who become brown Anglos equally destroy their integral personalities.

One of the most frustrating aspects of the Chicano movement comes from this loss of individuality and the sacrifice of the individual personality for *la raza*. From one perspective it seems that those who blindly accept the *raza* concept do so out of insecurity about being Mexican-Americans. They look for scapegoats to blame for their own failures; thus society and American racism become the simple answers to their simple minds.

In one respect the Chicanos are right: there is little knowledge, appreciation, and acceptance of their cultural heritage. For this the Anglo must accept responsibility. The Mexican-American has been taken for granted and has been rejected because of his differences. Until the Mexican-American, at least from the Anglo point of view, becomes more like the dominant society, he will be viewed as an inferior aberrant. This has been the traditional pattern of all ethnic groups in the United States. It is a pattern that requires changing.

True pluralism involves the acceptance of differences in cultural patterns and behavior. It is not a slavish acceptance of a particular point of view. One of the fundamental problems with Schools of Education lies in perpetuation of singular behavior patterns for all children, regardless of background and individual differences. New teachers need to be taught the diversity of American culture, not merely the aspects of the dominant Anglo component.

The Mexican-American, by the same token, has the responsibility of educating the Anglo. He can serve as the bridge between cultures. Yet the Frito Bandito was roundly condemned. Errant sensitivity sent the chubby little bandit into oblivion, and the knee jerk Anglo continues to pride himself on his tolerance. What the Mexican-American needs to do is shake hell out of a few liberal shibboleths and not become the complaisant tool of those who would manipulate him in order to assuage their conscience.

Bibliography

By no means is the following bibliography definitive. Frankly, if we consider the amount of stuff being published in so-called Chicano publications, it would border on the endless to prepare a complete bibliography on the Mexican-American. Therefore, a selective bibliography becomes the most convenient and expeditious way with which to acquaint the reader with the literature on a given subject.

Of course, the problem of bias rears its ugly head. Usually, bibliographies reflect the biases of the author. This one certainly does not make an exception to that general premise. To be sure, some works have been pitched in that totally disagree with my views, but that is merely to con the reader into believing that I am a terribly objective fellow who serves as nothing but a neutered recorder of historical data. If you believe that, go back to page 1 and start reading the whole damned thing again.

Have fun with these other works. By the time you get halfway through the bibliography perhaps the point of complexity vis-á-vis the Mexican-American will be made. Perhaps some of the ready shibboleths will be rattled and questioned. If that is the case, then I can relax and enjoy the mountains.

General Works on Mexico and Spanish Background

Alba, Victor. *The Mexicans.* New York: Frederick A. Praeger, Publishers, 1967.

Atkin, Ronald. *Revolution: Mexico, 1910-1920.* New York: John Day, Co., 1971.

Brandenberg, Frank. *The Making of Modern Mexico.* Englewood Cliffs: Prentice Hall, 1963.

Brenner, Anita. *Idols Behind Altars.* New York: Bible and Tannen, 1967.

Chevalier, François. *Land and Society in Colonial Mexico: The Great Hacienda.* Berkeley: University of California Press, 1963.

Gamio, Manuel. *Forjando Patria.* Mexico, D.F.: Editorial Porrúa, S.A., 1960 (First Edition, 1916).

Hamill, Jr., Hugh M. *Dictatorship in Spanish America.* New York: Alfred A. Knopf, 1966.

Hill, Larry D. *Emissaries to a Revolution: Woodrow Wilson's Executive Agents in Mexico.* Baton Rouge: Louisiana State University Press, 1973.

James, Daniel. *Mexico and the Americans.* New York: Frederick A. Praeger, Publishers, 1963.

Paz, Octavio. *El Laberinto de la Soledad.* Mexico: Fondo de Cultura Económica, 1957.

Paz, Octavio. *The Labyrinth of Solitude; life and tought in Mexico.* Translated by Lysander Kemp. New York: Grove Press, 1962.

Powell, Philip W. *Tree of Hate: Propaganda and Prejudice Affecting United States Relations with the Hispanic World.* New York: Basic Books, 1971.

Ramos, Samuel. *Perfil del hombre y la cultura en México.* 4th. ed. Mexico, D.F.: Universidad Nacional Autónoma de México, 1963 (First edition, 1934).

Ramos, Samuel. *Profile of man and culture in Mexico.* Translated by Peter G. Earl. Austin: University of Texas Press, 1962.

Simpson, Lesley Bird. *Many Mexicos.* Berkeley: University of California Press, 1966.

Whetten, Nathan L. *Rural Mexico.* Chicago: University of Chicago Press, 1948.

General Studies on Mexican-Americans and the Southwest

Acuña, Rodolfo. *Occupied America: The Chicano Struggle for Liberation.* San Francisco: Canfield Press, 1972.

Burman, John. *Mexican-Americans in the United States: A Reader.* Cambridge, Massachusetts: Schenkman Publishing Company, Inc., 1970.

Burman, John. *Documents of the Chicano Struggle.* New York: Pathfinder Press, 1971.

Gebler, Leo, Joan W. Moore, and Ralph C. Guzman. *The Mexican-American People: The Nation's Second Largest Minority.* New York: Greenwood Press, 1968.

Harth, Dorothy E., and Lewis M. Baldwin. (eds.) *Voices of Aztlán: Chicano Literature of Today*. New York: New American Library, 1974.

Higham, John. *Strangers in the Land: Patterns of American Nativism, 1860-1925*. New York: Atheneum, 1955.

Hollon, W. Eugene. *The Southwest: Old and New*. Lincoln: University of Nebraska Press, 1968.

Horgan, Paul. *Great River: The Rio Grande in North American History*. 2 vols. New York: Rinehart, 1954.

Lamar, Howard Roberts. *The Far Southwest: 1846-1912: A Territorial History*. New York: W. W. Norton, Co., 1970.

Landes, Ruth. *Latin-Americans of the Southwest*. New York: McGraw-Hill, 1965.

Ludwig, Ed and James Santibañez. *The Chicanos: Mexican-American Voices*. Baltimore: Penguin Books, 1971.

Machado, Manuel A., Jr., "Chicano Studies: A Mexican American Dissents," *University Bookman*, Fall, 1970.

Machado, Manuel A., Jr., "Mexican-American History: Problems and Prospects," *Western Review*, Winter, 1971.

McWilliams, Carey. *North From Mexico: The Spanish Speaking People in the United States*. New York: Greenwood Press, 1968.

Madsen, William. *Mexican-Americans of South Texas*. San Francisco: Holt, Rinehart, and Winston, 1964.

Meier, Matt S. and Feliciano Rivera. *The Chicanos: A History of Mexican Americans*. New York: Hill and Wang, 1972.

Meinig, D.W. *Southwest: Three Peoples in Geographical Change, 1600-1970*. New York: Oxford University Press, 1971.

Moquín, Wayne (ed.). *A Documentary History of the Mexican American*. New York: Frederick A. Praeger, Publishers, 1971.

Newman, Patty. *Do It Up Brown*. San Diego: View Point Books, 1971.

Robinson, Cecil, "Spring Water with a Taste of the Land," *American West.* Summer, 1966.

Rowan, Helen, "A Minority Nobody Knows," *Atlantic.* June, 1967.

Samora, Julián (ed.). *La Raza: The Forgotten Americans* Notre Dame: University of Notre Dame Press, 1966.

Servín, Manuel P. (ed.). *The Mexican-Americans: An Awakening Minority.* Beverly Hills: Glencoe Press, 1970.

Simmen, Edward. (ed.). *The Chicano: From Caricature to Self-Portrait.* New York: New American Library, 1971.

Simmen, Edward. *Pain and Promise: The Chicano Today.* New York: New American Library, 1972.

Weber, David S. (ed.). *Foreigners in Their Native Land: Historical Roots of the Mexican American.* Albuquerque: University of New Mexico Press, 1973.

Specialized Works
on Mexican-Americans

Alvarez, José Hernández. "A Demographic Profile on the Mexican Immigration to the United States, 1910-1950," *Journal of International Studies.* July, 1966.

Campa, Arthur L. *Treasure of the Sangre de Cristos: Tales and Traditions of the Spanish Southwest.* Norman: University of Oklahoma Press, 1963.

Campeán, Mario, José Angel Gutiérrez, and Antonio Camejo. *La Raza Unida Party in Texas.* New York: Pathfinder Press, 1970.

Castañeda, Carlos E., trans. *The Mexican Side of the Texan Revolution.* Dallas: P.L. Turner, C. 1928.

Clark, Margaret. *Health in the Mexican-American Culture.* Berkeley: University of California Press, 1959.

Cleland, Robert G. *The Cattle on a Thousand Hills: Southern California, 1850-1870.* San Marino, California: The Huntington Library, 1941.

Corwin, Arthur M., "Mexican-American History: An Assessment," *Pacific Historical Review*. August, 1973.

Cue Canovas, Agustín. *Los Estados Unidos y el México Olvidado*. Mexico, D.F.: B. Costa-Amic, 1970.

D'Antonio, William V. and William H. Form. *Influentials in Two Border Cities: A Study in Community Decision-Making*. Notre Dame: University of Notre Dame Press, 1965.

De Toledano, Ralph. *Little César.* Washington: Anthem Books, 1971.

Dobie, J. Frank, ed. *Puro Mexicano*. Austin: Texas Folklore Society, 1935.

Dobie, J. Frank. *Tongues of the Monte*. Garden City, New York: Doubleday, Doran and Co., 1935.

Dunne, John Gregory. *Delano: The Story of the Grape Strike*. New York: Farrar, Strauss, and Giroux, 1967.

Galarza, Ernesto. *Merchants of Labor: The Mexican Bracero Story*. San Jose, California: The Rosicrucian Press, 1964.

Galarza, Ernesto. *Spiders in the House and Workers in the Field*. Notre Dame: University of Notre Dame Press, 1970.

Galarza, Ernesto. *Strangers in Our Fields*. Washington, D.C.: Joint United States-Mexico Trade Union Committee, 1956.

Galarza, Ernesto, Herman Gallegos, and Julián Samora. *Mexican Americans in the Southwest*. Santa Barbara: McNally and Loftin, 1969.

Gamio, Manuel. *Mexican Immigration to the United States*. Chicago: University of Chicago Press, 1930.

Gamio, Manuel. *The Mexican Immigrant, His Life Story. Autobiographic Documents Collected by Manuel Gamio*. Chicago: University of Chicago Press, 1931.

Gardner, Richard. *GRITO!* New York: Bobbs-Merrill Co., 1970.

González, Nancie L. *The Spanish American of New Mexico: A Distinctive Heritage*. Mexican American Study Project Advance Report 9. Los Angeles, Division of Research,

Graduate School of Business, University of California, 1967.

Heller, Celia S. *Mexican-American Youth: Forgotten Youth at the Cross Roads.* New York: Random House, 1969.

Jenkinson, Michael. *Tijerina: Land Grant Conflict in New Mexico.* Albuquerque: Paisano Press, 1968.

Kiev, Ari. *Curanderismo: Mexican-American Folk Psychiatry.* New York: The Free Press, 1968.

Knowlton, Clark S. "Patrón-Peón Patterns Among the Spanish Americans of New Mexico," *Social Forces.* October, 1962.

Manuel, Herschel T. *Spanish-Speaking Children of the Southwest.* Austin: University of Texas Press, 1965.

Matthiessen, Peter. *Sal Si Puedes: César Chávez and the New American Revolution.* New York: Delta Books, 1969.

Nabokov, Peter. *Tijerina and the Court House Raid.* Albuquerque: University of New Mexico Press, 1963.

Paredes, Americo. *With His Pistol in His Hand—A Border Ballad and Its Hero.* Austin: University of Texas Press, 1958.

Peñalosa, Fernando, "The Changing Mexican-American in Southern California," *Sociology and Social Research.* September, 1967.

Peñalosa, Fernando and Edward C. McDonagh, "Education, Economic Status, and Social Class Awareness of Mexican Americans," *Phylon.* Summer, 1968.

Pitt, Leonard. *The Decline of the Californios: A Social History of the Spanish-Speaking Californians, 1848-1890.* Berkeley: University of California Press, 1970.

Robinson, Cecil. *With the Ears of Strangers: The Mexican in American Literature.* Tucson: University of Arizona Press, 1963.

Romano V., Octavio Ignacio, "Charismatic Medicine, Faith Healing, and Sainthood," *American Anthropologist.* October, 1965.

Romano V., Octavio Ignacio, "Donship in a Mexican Ameri-

can Community in Texas," *American Anthropologist.*
December, 1960.

Rubel, J. Arthur. *Across the Tracks: Mexican-Americans in a Texas City.* Austin: University of Texas Press, 1966.

Rubel, J. Arthur, "Concepts of Disease in Mexican-American Culture," *American Anthropologist.* October, 1960.

Sánchez, George I. *Forgotten People: A Study of New Mexicans.* Albuquerque: University of New Mexico Press, 1940.

Gringa y chicano

Tee hee!

Joseph's

Index

Agricultural Workers' Organizing Committee, 99
Agriculture, condition of, 66
Alianza Federal de los Pueblos Libres, 112
Alianza Federal de Mercedes, 110-11
American Revolution, 20-21
Apodaca, Jerry, 180-81
Archdiocese of Los Angeles, 162
Article 27, 63
Austin, Stephen F., 25
Aztecs, 4

Baca, Elfego, 44
Barrios, 116-17
Bilingualism, 128-29
Bracero program, 76-79, 87, 88, 90
Bonaparte, Napoleon, 21

Bonney, William "Billie the Kid," 43-44
Bourbon reforms, 18-19

California: Constitution of 1849, 33;
economic expansion of, 42 ff.;
Gold Rush, 32-33;
liberalism in, 27-28;
social structure of, 20;
statehood, 33
Californios, 29
Cannery and Agricultural Workers Industrial Union, 70, 71
Cárdenas, Lázaro, 68
Carranza, Venustiano, 52, 55-58, 63
Cart War, 36

Casa chica, 13
Castro, Raúl, 180-81
Cattle industry, Mexican influence on, 42-43
Centralists, 24
Charles II, 17-18
Chávez, César Estrada: charisma of, 98-99;
as Community Service Organizer, 99;
fast of, 104-6;
incarceration of, 102;
as propagandist, 103-4
Chicano, 170
Chicano studies, 138, 142-43
"Chico and the Man," 180
Civil Rights Acts, 131
Columbus, Christopher, 2
Comparative history, 142
Confederación de Uniones de Campesinos y Obreros Mexicanos, 70
Confederación de Uniones Mexicanas, 69
Condederación Regional de Obreros Mexicanos, 69
Constitution of 1917, 57
Cortés, Hernán, 2-3
Cortina, Juan Nepomuceno "Cheno," 36
Court of Private Land Claims, 45-46
Crystal City, Texas, 172
Cultural transference, 154-58
Culture, deterioration of, 117-19

Delano, 99-102
De las Casas, Bartolomé, 8, 10
Del Valle, Reginaldo, 58-60

De Portolá, Gaspar, 19
Díaz, Felíx, 55
Díaz, Porfirio, 47-48, 52, 53
Donship, 165-66
Doña Marina, 3-4

Emigrés, 61
Encomenderos, 7
Encomienda system, 6-7
England, 10-13

Federalists, 24
Filibusters, 22
French Revolution, 21
Frito Bandito, 178

Gadsden Purchase, 30, 38-39
GI Bill, 85
González, Henry B., 120-21
González, Rodolfo "Corky," 171
Gorras Blancas, 45
Great Crash, 67
Guadalupe Hidalgo, Treaty of, 31-32, 107-8

Hacienda system, 9
Henry VIII, 10
Hitler, Adolf, 73
Huerta, Victoriano, 52, 55, 62
Huitzilopochtli, 4

Iberian Peninsula, invasion of, 2
Illegal immigrants, 88, 89, 90
Immigration acts, 65
Immigration, restrictions on 66-67
Inquisition, 11
Iturbide, Agustín de, 24

Juárez, Benito, 39-40

Kennedy, John F., 121-22
Kino, Eusebio, 17

Labor, Mexican source of, 64-65
La causa, 138
Lamy, Jean Baptiste, Bishop of
    New Mexico, 46
L'Archeveque, Sostenes, 44
League of United Latin American
    Citizens, 86-87
Lincoln County War, 43-44
L ó p e z   T i j e r i n a ,   R e i e s :
    background of, 109;
    as charismatic leader, 125;
    conflict with SCLC, 126;
    incarceration of, 114
Louisiana Purchase, 22

McCarran-Walter Immigration
    Act, 91-92
Madero, Francisco, 52-55
Mano Negra, 45
Martínez, Fr. José Antonio, 38, 46
Mayas, 4
Mestizo, 13
Mexican-American nationalism,
    169-70
Mexican   American   Political
    Association, 86
Mexican   American   Youth
    Organization, 172
Mexico: French invasion of, 36;
    independence of, 22-23
Mexican Revolution, 52-61
Mexican War, 29-30
Miscengenation, 13, 14
Muñoz, Rosalío, 144-45

Murietta, Joaquín, 34

National   Chicano   Moratorium,
    145-46
National Farm Workers Associa-
    tion, 98
National forests, 108
New Laws of the Indies, 8
New Mexico, 16, 37, 44
New Spain, 6 ff.

Old Spanish Days, 15-16
Orozco, Pascual, Jr., 53, 54, 62
Oñate, Juan de, 16

Pachuco riots, 83-84
Pachucos, 80-84
Patria chica, 158
Patrón-peón relationship, 7, 47
Paz, Octavio, 136-37
Penitentes, 46
Plan de Ayala, 54
Plan Espiritual de Aztlán, 170-71
Plan de San Luis Potosí, 52, 53
Poinsett, Joel R., 24
Political Association of Spanish
    Speaking Organizations, 86
Political organization, problems
    of, 166-68
Prohibition, 63-64
Protestant reformation, 10
Provincias Internas, 19
Public Law 45, 76
Pueblo Revolt, 16

Quetzalcoatl, 5

Raza Unida Party, 172
Religious practices, 160-62

Repatriation program, 68-69
Ricos, 36-37
Río Arriba, 112-13
Roman Catholicism, 162-64
Roosevelt, Franklin Delano, 68

Sánchez, Alfonso, 110, 111-12
Sánchez, George I., 127-28
San Juan-Chama Diversion Project, 112
Salazar, Rubén, 146-49
Santa Anna, Antonio López de, 25-27
Santa Fe Ring, 45-46
Serra, Junípero, 20
Sheep industry, 43
Sinarquismo, 84
Sleepy Lagoon Case, 81-83
Sleepy Lagoon Defense Committee, 82
Social mobility, 116-17
Social Workers, meddlesome nature of, 129, 131-32
Southwest, economic expansion of, 42 ff.

Taos Rebellion, 37
Teamsters Union, 101-3
Teatro Campesino, 173
Texas, 25, 27, 43
Third World, 179

United Farm Workers Organizing Committee, 99
United Leagues, 90-91
United States Armed Forces, 75-76
United States, neutrality of, 73
University of Montana, 143-44

Villa, Francisco "Pancho," 52, 53, 57
Virgin of Guadalupe, 6-7
Viva Wallace Movement, 123

War of Reform, 39
War of Spanish Succession, 18
Wilson, Woodrow, 58
World War II, 73-74, 76

Zapata, Emiliano, 53